No Clear and Present Danger

*the text of this book is printed
on 100% recycled paper*

Books by Bruce M. Russett

Community and Contention: Britain and America in the Twentieth Century (1963)

World Handbook of Political and Social Indicators (principal author, 1964)

Trends in World Politics (1965)

World Politics in the General Assembly (coauthor, 1965)

International Regions and the International System (1967)

Economic Theories of International Politics (editor, 1968)

What Price Vigilance? The Burdens of National Defense (1970)

No Clear and Present Danger: A Skeptical View of the United States Entry into World War II (1972)

Peace, War, and Numbers (editor, 1972)

No Clear and Present Danger

A Skeptical View of the United States Entry into World War II

BRUCE M. RUSSETT

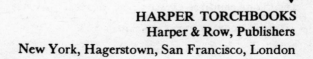

HARPER TORCHBOOKS
Harper & Row, Publishers
New York, Hagerstown, San Francisco, London

First TORCHBOOK edition published 1972.

LIBRARY OF CONGRESS CATALOG CARD NUMBER: 79-178973

STANDARD BOOK NUMBER: 06-131649-0

Designed by C. Linda Dingler

77 78 79 80   12 11 10 9 8 7 6 5

For Mark and Daniel
No foreign wars for them

Contents

There is no guarantee whatsoever that there would be any better history written should we participate again to bring complete victory to one side . . . Great as is the power of America, we cannot police Europe, much less Asia, and in addition protect the whole Western Hemisphere . . . Nor can we expect that a nation having as many unsolved problems as we have, and as little understanding of some of the problems that lie beyond our borders, would be given, under the all-embracing hysteria of war, wisdom for the perfect solution of all the world's ills.

Norman Thomas, 1940

The one great danger we face is that we may overcommit ourselves in this battle against Russia . . . An unwise and overambitious foreign policy, and particularly the effort to do more than we are able to do, is the one thing which might in the end destroy our armies and prove a real threat to the liberty of the people of the United States.

Robert A. Taft, 1951

Preface

It has been a long trip, and is not yet complete. Nevertheless I have come far enough to want to give a report on the vivid scenery to be viewed from this prospect. I began, as a child in World War II, with a firm hatred of the Axis powers and a conviction that America was fighting for its very existence. After the war, Stalinist Russia merely replaced Hitlerite Germany as the insatiable aggressor. With most Americans I accepted without much question the need for active resistance to Communism, and the necessity that such resistance would often have to be military in character. Though as a young scholar I did become very concerned about arms control and the risks of nuclear war, my faith in the requirement for military assistance to threatened members of the Free World remained essentially unshaken. I was fairly hawkish on Vietnam, and saw only in early 1967 that the war had been a mistake. In retrospect, I am not proud of having taken so long. Even then, I considered that the sole mistake was having chosen a conflict where the essential conditions of victory were absent.

In the past few years, however, I have slowly begun to question my earlier easy assumptions. Once some began to fall, others became far less tenable. Here really was a row of intellectual dominoes. If Vietnam was unnecessary or wrong, then where else? How distorted were our images of the origins of the cold war? What has been the role of economic interests in promoting foreign involvements by the United States government?

This is an exciting time in which to be a scholar. Some of these questions were forced on me directly by observing events; others were in substantial part impelled by the questioning of students who had been less thoroughly indoctrinated in the cold war myths than I, and thus rejected them more easily. In this reexamination I am, of course not alone. Many Americans of all generations have come to question their former assumptions. Still, the results differ among us. I find the New Left's emphasis on foreign investment and trade interests to be stimulating and overdue; in the anti-Communist hysteria of the first cold war decades such matters were all too thoroughly ignored. Nevertheless I am still unconvinced that such influences should be elevated to the role of a primary explanation, and while in this book I sometimes suggest their relevance to pre-World War II policy preferences I do not emphasize them. But I am interested in the work of others on these questions, and consider them with a mind more open than before.

And although there are finally some rumblings on the New Left, and occasionally elsewhere, about the propriety of American participation in World War II, they have yet to surface much in public. The situation is curious. A few writers, I among them,[1] challenged the prevailing interpretation about war with Japan some time ago, but with little impact beyond a small circle of professional scholars. Participation in the war against Hitler remains almost wholly sacrosanct, nearly in the realm of theology. Yet it seems to me that many of the arguments against other wars can also be applied, with somewhat less force, to this one too. Hence I came to rethink, and to write while still in the process of rethinking.

For the opportunity to reconsider my old myths I am grateful to a year in Brussels, made possible by a fellowship from

1. See my article, "Pearl Harbor: Deterrence Theory and Decision Theory," *Journal of Peace Research* I (1967): 89–105, parts of which are reproduced here. Parts of Chapter 5 are taken from my "A Macroscopic View of International Politics," in Vincent Davis, Maurice East and James Rosenau, eds., *The Analysis of International Politics* (New York: Free Press, 1971). All materials are reprinted with permission.

the John Simon Guggenheim Memorial Foundation and a Fulbright-Hays award. I neither expected nor intended to spend much time on these matters when the awards were made, but such things will happen when a scholar is given time for reflection. A decision-maker and a scholar helped unintentionally. The process surfaced on the night President Nixon announced the American foray into Cambodia, which I absorbed under the influence of just having read the late Richard Hofstadter's essay on Charles A. Beard's attitudes toward the war that was approaching over a generation ago.

Many colleagues, friends, and students made more deliberate contributions by giving their reactions to my early thoughts. Notably helpful were John Morton Blum, Robert H. Ferrell, Glenn May, Paul Hammond, Douglas Rae, James Patrick Sewell, Fred Sondermann, Gaddis Smith, John Sullivan, and H. Bradford Westerfield. My wife, Cynthia Eagle Russett, as so often, played a crucial role in the initial stages by providing both insights and stimulating criticism. Wendell Bell urged me to rescue the first version of this essay from the obscurity of a scholarly journal. Even more carefully than is customary, however, I want to absolve anyone from responsibility for the opinions I express here.

B. M. R.

Hamden, Connecticut
May 1971

No Clear and Present Danger

1

Isolationism Old and New

The "lessons" of history

Whatever criticisms of twentieth-century American foreign policy are put forth, United States participation in World War II remains almost entirely immune. According to our national mythology, that was a "good war," one of the few for which the benefits clearly outweighed the costs. Except for a few books published shortly after the war and quickly forgotten, this orthodoxy has been essentially unchallenged.[1] The isolationists stand discredited, and "isolationist" remains a useful pejorative with which to tar the opponents of American intervention in foreign lands.

Such virtual unanimity on major policy matters is rare. World War I long ago came under the revisionists' scrutiny. The origins of the cold war have been challenged more recently, with many people asking whether the Soviet-American conflict was primarily the result of Russian aggressiveness or even whether it was the inevitable consequence of throwing together "two scorpions in a bottle." But all orthodoxy ought

1. For a few years the now-prevailing orthodoxy had not yet crystallized, and a substantial minority of the American population remained skeptical. For example, a Gallup poll in October 1947 asked, "Do you think it was a mistake for the United States to enter World War II?" The response was No 66%, Yes 24%, No Answer 10%. Reported in Hazel Erskine, "The Polls: Is War a Mistake?" *Public Opinion Quarterly* 34, no. 1 (Spring 1970): 137.

to be confronted occasionally, whether the result be to destroy, revise, or reincarnate old beliefs. Furthermore, this does seem an auspicious time to reexamine the standard credo about participation in World War II. Interventionism is again being questioned and Americans are groping toward a new set of principles to guide their foreign policy. Where should we intervene and where withdraw; where actively to support a "balance of power" and where husband our resources? A reexamination of the World War II experience is deliberately a look at a limiting case—an effort to decide whether, in the instance where the value of intervention is most widely accepted, the interventionist argument really is so persuasive. We should consider the World War II experience not because intervention was obvious folly, but indeed because the case for American action there is strong.

I do *not*, of course, argue that one can readily generalize from the choices of 1941 to those of 1950 or 1970. The world has changed, and many of the favorable conditions that once made isolationism or "continentalism" a plausible policy to some have vanished, perhaps forever. I feel ambivalent about the contemporary meaning of the theme developed here, in view of the manifest changes of the past 30 years and the more or less "internationalist" policy preferences that I have shared with most Americans for many years. But almost all of us do on occasion invoke the "lessons" of Manchuria, Munich, the Spanish Civil War, or Pearl Harbor; or for that matter Rome and Carthage or the Peloponnesian Wars. We therefore owe it to ourselves to look critically at this historical experience, too. I think the theme of this essay needs stating even at the risk that some people may apply it inappropriately.

Furthermore, a new look at World War II is in some real sense merely an extension of arguments that have been raised against contemporary American intervention in Southeast Asia. The intervention has been justified both on moral grounds—the need to save a small country from communist dictatorship, and on strategic grounds of American self-interest—the need to prop up dominoes and prevent the extension of a hostile power's sphere of influence.

And the opponents of that intervention have included among their arguments some that recall the debates of 1941: America cannot be the world's policeman stepping in to halt everything we might consider to be aggression or to resist governments whose philosophies or policies we consider repugnant. Nor from a pure self-interest viewpoint would such critics accept our action in South Vietnam. It is a small country, far away. Its entire national income is equivalent only to the normal *growth* of the United States national income in a single month. Communist rule in that state, or even in its immediate neighbors as well, would make but an insignificant difference to the global balance of power. In any case, the forces of nationalism render very dubious an assumption that a Communist government would represent a dependable long-term gain for China or Russia.

Thus, in an important way the record of discussion in 1940 and 1941 is being replayed now. Opponents of contemporary intervention may well find ammunition by pointing out the inflated nature of the interventionists' rhetoric preceding World War II. If in the cold light of the seventies the original arguments seem excessive, then how much more misleading must be the recent versions? Or on the contrary, if a man is sure that the Southeast Asian operation was a mistake, can he still justify the World War II experience? Perhaps his continued acceptance of the latter should cause him to rethink his extreme opposition to the American interventions of the last decade.

An unnecessary war

The theme of this brief book should already be apparent, but I will state it explicitly here before going further: American participation in World War II had very little effect on the essential *structure* of international politics thereafter, and probably did little either to advance the material welfare of most Americans or to make the nation secure from foreign military threats (the presumed goals of advocates of a "realist" foreign policy). (By structure I mean the basic balance of forces in the world, regardless of which particular nations are powerful vis-a-vis the United States.) In fact, most Americans probably would have been no worse off, and possibly a little better, if the United States had never become a belligerent. Russia replaced Germany as the great threat to European security, and Japan, despite its territorial losses, is once more a major power. The war was not clearly a mistake as most of us now consider the Vietnam War to have been. Yet it may well have been an unnecessary war that did little for us and that we need not have fought. Moreover, it set some precedents for our thinking that led too easily to later interventions—interventions that might have been challenged more quickly and more effectively in the absence of such vivid memories of World War II.

We shall first review the events in Europe and the North Atlantic which led to widespread sentiment that Hitler had to be opposed by whatever means were necessary. We must both confront the strategic arguments and consider on what grounds strategy could be subordinated to moral conviction that Nazism had to be deposed. Next we must look at what transpired in the Pacific, since many Americans still believe that while war with Nazi Germany was in large part by American initiative, we had no choice with Japan. After all, the United States was attacked at Pearl Harbor. Why then agonize over the question whether war with the Japanese was desirable? We shall then examine more closely some of the parallels, in the process of decision-making and in the arguments employed, between intervention in World War II and recent American interventions justified by cold war analyses, and close by asking what other perspectives might have avoided error both then and more recently.

Many readers surely will be uncomfortable with the book's theme, and even offended by it. For example, it can hardly be easy for a man who spent two or three of his prime years fighting World War II to think that his sacrifice had little point. Moreover, the moral outrage against Nazism that we all share makes it difficult to separate ethics from an objective assessment of the threat Germany and Japan actually posed to American national security. To suggest that the two must be kept *analytically* distinct—even if in the end one sees the former as justifying intervention after all—is to risk being considered at least a first cousin of the Beast of Belsen.

Yet it is precisely moral considerations that demand a re-examination of our World War II myths. Social scientists have accepted too many assumptions uncritically. Too few Americans, especially government officials, really looked very hard at their beliefs about the origins of the cold war before about five years ago, or seriously considered "economic" interpretations of foreign policy. Recently, however, we have been illuminated as well as blinded by an occasion we could not ignore. On watching the fireball at Alamogordo in 1945 Robert Oppenheimer mused, "I am become death, destroyer of worlds." Vietnam has been to social scientists what Alamogordo was to the physicists. Few of those who have observed it can easily return to their comfortable presumptions about America's duty, or right, to fight in distant lands.

One serious problem in reevaluating American foreign policy before World War II stems from its distance in time. How do we treat the knowledge we gain from actually observing the intervening thirty years? Is it fair to judge the friends and opponents of Franklin Roosevelt with the advantages of 20-20 hindsight? Certainly we must keep separate what they knew or could have known, and what was unavoidably hidden from them. From captured documents we now see more clearly the motivations of some Axis leaders than contemporaries could have; we know with just what strength the Soviet Union emerged in Central Europe after the elimination of German power. If they exaggerated the then-present danger how can we be too condemning?

Nevertheless, the purpose in reconsidering World War II is not to judge, but to learn. In retaining our own humility it is fair to insist on a degree of humility in our leaders of all

eras. Many of those who advocated war against Germany and
Japan were very sure of themselves and their visions; the
same could be said of many "cold warriors." They supported
acts which left millions dead and changed all our lives. Some
considered Hitler not only a devil, but to have near God-like
powers enabling him to walk across the water to North America. The "yellow horde" was ready to invade from the other
side; I remember being told how the Japanese coveted California. Both recall more recent images of the Russians as
ten feet tall. In fact, our alleged vulnerability to the Axis
threat was often used to justify continued involvement and
active opposition to apparent Soviet expansionism in the postwar world. Without seeking judgment or scapegoats, perhaps we still can learn by identifying even the most excusable
errors of others.

My intention here is to be provocative and not to set forth
revealed truth. The argument is not one subject to the principles of measurement and the strict canons of hypothesis-
testing—the mode of inquiry with which I feel most comfortable. Nevertheless the subject is too important to leave
untouched simply because the whole battery of modern social
science cannot be brought to bear on it. Similarly, there is an
intellectual dialectic, driven by the need of most thinkers to
relate their ideas to established thought patterns, that requires a new view to be stated forcefully and one-sidedly.
Hamlets do not make revolutions. Hence we shall proceed
to the argument, though the reader—and sometimes the
writer too—will doubtless have reservations.

Although I have tried to give some evidence to support the
more controversial statements of fact, full documentation
would be out of place in such an essay. The need is not to
uncover new facts from the archives, but to look again at the
old facts from a different perspective. Some of my interpretations will be challengeable, and many readers may decide
that despite my arguments the war still was worthwhile. Any
retrospective analysis of "might-have-beens" is subject to all
the perils of conjecture. We more or less know what *did* hap-

pen as a result of American participation in the war, and can only speculate on what would otherwise have happened. But that reservation cuts two ways, since those who will disagree with this book's interpretations are also forced into speculation.

In any case, I think defenders of American intervention will find that their case ultimately rests on other, and less confident, grounds than most have previously accepted. I suspect that no reader will ever again view World War II in quite the same way as before. A new look should at least clear aside many previous exaggerations of the kind of threat foreign powers could then and now present to the United States.

2

The Impending Stalemate
in Europe

The illusive victory

American participation in World War II brought the country
few gains; the United States was no more secure at the end
than it could have been had it stayed out. First, let us look at
the "might have beens" in Europe. The standard justification
of American entry into the war is that otherwise Germany
would have reigned supreme on the continent, victor over
Russia and Britain. With all the resources of Europe at the
disposal of his totalitarian government, plus perhaps parts of
the British fleet, Hitler would have posed an intolerable threat
to the security of the United States. He could have consoli-
dated his winnings, built his war machine, established bridge-
heads in South America, and ultimately could and likely
would have moved against North America to achieve world
domination.

Several links in this argument might deserve scrutiny, but
by far the critical one is the first, that Hitler would have won
World War II. Such a view confuses the ability of Germany's
enemies to *win* with their ability to achieve a *stalemate*. Also,
it tends to look more at the military-political situation of
June 1940 than at that of December 1941, and to confuse
President Roosevelt's decision to aid Britain (and later
Russia) by "all measures short of war" with an actual American declaration of war. Let me say clearly: I basically accept

the proposition that German domination of all Europe, with Britain and Russia prostrate, would have been intolerable to the United States. By any of the classical conceptions of "power-balancing" and "national interest," the United States should indeed have intervened if necessary to prevent that outcome.

For a while it appeared American intervention might quickly become essential. The Hitler-Stalin pact of August 1939 guaranteed Germany against any Soviet interference, and made the attack on Poland militarily safe. Poland fell before the *Wehrmacht* in 27 days. After a lull during the winter, in the spring of 1940 German armies invaded and quickly conquered Denmark, Norway, Belgium, and the Netherlands. France surrendered in less than two and a half months. Most of the British expeditionary force to the continent escaped at Dunkirk, but its heavy equipment was left behind. Mussolini finally felt sure enough of the outcome to enter the war just a few days before the fall of France. Hitler began preparation for Operation Sea Lion, the invasion of Britain.

But then the machine halted, and prospects changed. By the end of 1941 Hitler had already lost his gamble to control Europe. In large part this was due to British skill, courage, and good luck in the summer of 1940. Given German naval inferiority, Hitler had to destroy the British air force for an invasion to be possible. But the RAF won the Battle of Britain and Hitler decided against undertaking Operation Sea Lion; it was too risky.[1] From that point onward German relative capabilities for a cross-channel attack declined rather than improved. The ebb of the tide against Hitler was very greatly assisted, as an absolutely essential condition, by American military and economic assistance to the British.

Recall American initiatives during the first two years of

1. In fact there is reason to believe that Hitler never had much faith in Sea Lion, recognizing the great hurdles in its way. See F. M. Sallagar, *The Road to Total War: Escalation in World War II* (Santa Monica, California: Rand Corporation, R-465-PR, 1969), pp. 68–80.

war in Europe. In the fall of 1939 the Neutrality Act was amended to repeal the arms embargo and make any goods available to all belligerents on a cash-and-carry basis. Thanks to the British fleet, only the Allies could take advantage of this measure. The destroyers-for-bases exchange with Britain was agreed upon in September 1940. Many of the old American warships were of doubtful military value, but the trade's symbolism was extremely significant. The Lend-Lease Act, which was to pour billions of dollars of supplies into Britain and, beginning later, to Russia, was signed in March 1941. In July 1941 United States forces occupied Iceland and President Roosevelt had agreed that American ships would escort convoys—including British ships—as far as Iceland. Convoying meant that if German U-boats approached the American escorts were to "shoot on sight" to insure that the goods got through. These steps played central roles in British survival. By August Roosevelt and Churchill could meet in a cruiser off Argentia, Newfoundland to discuss military collaboration and, with the Atlantic Charter, to begin planning for the postwar world.

I do not, therefore, argue that American nonbelligerent assistance to Britain was a mistake, quite the contrary. Yet that is just the point—by the end of 1941 Britain's survival was essentially assured. She might lose some colonies, her world position would be weakened, perhaps in the long run her independent existence would be threatened by the Germans in a second round of war. For the immediate future, nevertheless, Britain would live. Indeed, such a conclusion helps to make sense of Hitler's daring gamble in attacking Russia in the late spring of 1941. The British had made it through the worst patch, and only by a long and mutually-exhausting war could Germany hope to wear them down. At the least, German hopes for a quick end to the war had been irretrievably lost.

If British survival into 1941 raised the specter of deadlock or war of attrition to Hitler, the failure of his attack on Russia brought the specter to life. He had intended to invade the Soviet Union in mid-May 1941, but things had not gone well. His ally, Mussolini, had invaded Greece and met with repeated defeats. Hitler felt obliged to divert German troops from the Russian front to rescue the Italians and the German flank. His invasion of Russia, Operation Barbarossa, was thus delayed five weeks until June 22 when, without ultimatum or declaration of war, the troops moved east.

The attack itself was an admission that the war against Britain had gone badly. By some interpretations the German invasion of Russia was an attempt to secure the resources, especially oil, necessary to bring the British down in a long war of attrition; by others it was an effort to strike the Russians at a time of Hitler's choosing rather than wait for the Russians to come in on the British side later. Surely the prospect of being the weight in balance at the key moment would have been greatly tempting to Stalin. By either interpretation the attack accepted great risks, and was the last try with any hope of success to seize a clear victory.

With the onset of the Russian winter and Hitler's inability to take Moscow—Napoleon had at least managed that—the prospect of German failure was sharp. Looking back, we now can see that *this* was in fact the hinge of fate; the more visible turning a year later was more nearly the outward sign of a predetermined shift. A man's health declines from the onset of fatal disease, not from the moment of medical diagnosis. The battle of Stalingrad in late 1942 marked the final, visible blunting of Hitler's drive to the east, and from then on the military initiative was in Soviet hands. Even at the beginning of the invasion the Russians were superior not only in manpower resources, but in tanks and even planes; the principal difference was the initially far-superior German organization.[2] During the first year of the war in Russia German military production figures were only about one-fourth of what they had been in 1918; in aircraft, trucks, armored

2. William L. Langer and S. Everett Gleason, *The Undeclared War, 1940–1941* (New York: Harper & Row, 1953), p. 533.

vehicles, artillery, and naval armaments German production was less than Britain's.[3] Despite widespread assumptions that the Nazis would win easily, by early-August 1941 Roosevelt was receiving reports, especially one from Harry Hopkins which he regarded highly, that the Russians would hold out.

The essential point is that the Russian success, like the British, occurred quite independently of American military action. During the early years of the war the quantity of supplies reaching Russia from the Western Hemisphere was not great; some would surely have gone there during 1942 whether or not the United States was a formal belligerent, just as they were going in substantial measure to Britain during 1941. By the middle of 1942 approximately half of the supplies had been sent by Britain. Some of the American shipments had begun while the United States was still formally neutral and most of the rest would doubtless have been sent even in the event of continued military neutrality.[4]

It seems most unlikely that the marginal increment that can be attributed to American *belligerency* in 1942 was critical to the Russian war effort. Certainly no allied military action in the west drew significant German forces away from the eastern campaign. At conferences with Roosevelt and Churchill, Stalin insisted that he did not regard the North African campaign as the second front he wanted to distract the Nazis. As evidenced by actual American conduct of the war in 1942, the immediate rescue of Russia was not the main purpose. American active participation surely shortened the conflict considerably, and very probably was the *sine qua non* for any clear-cut victory over the Nazis such as did occur. But for the more narrow purpose of maintaining British and

3. See Albert Speer, *Inside the Third Reich* (New York: Macmillan, 1970), p. 213, and Burton Klein, *Germany's Economic Preparations for War* (Cambridge: Harvard University Press, 1959), esp. p. 99.
4. See Herbert Feis, *Roosevelt, Churchill, Stalin* (Princeton, New Jersey: Princeton University Press, 1957), p. 78. Robert Huhn Jones, *The Roads to Russia; United States Lend-Lease to the Soviet Union* (Norman: University of Oklahoma Press, 1969) contends that although quantitatively not great, the particular composition of American aid may have been critical.

Soviet independence as centers of resistance to Germany, it is much harder to make a convincing case for the necessity of American belligerency.

Restraints in the naval war

What then would have been the most likely outcome had the United States remained formally neutral while shipping arms and economic assistance to Germany's opponents? First, it seems very unlikely that Hitler would have declared war on the United States. True, he did feel provoked by American naval action against German forces in the North Atlantic. In the autumn of 1941 American warships were escorting American and British freighters with orders to destroy any German submarines or raiders encountered. Yet even then Hitler instructed his submarines to protect themselves, but to instigate no attacks on American shipping. He would deal with this problem only later, after Russia had been beaten. Germany had lost one war by bringing America in against it. The Tripartite Pact with Italy and Japan declared that the members, "undertake to assist one another with all political, economic, and military means, if one of the three Contracting Parties is attacked by a Power at present not involved in the European War or in the Chinese-Japanese conflict." Despite naval action that he might have interpreted as attack, Hitler made no attempt to invoke the alliance. American "aid short of war" to the allies was surely less damaging to the Axis than active participation would be.[5]

5. Among the many proponents of the generally-held opinion that Hitler wanted badly to avoid war with the United States at this stage are Paul W. Schroeder, *The Axis Alliance and Japanese-American Relations, 1941* (Ithaca, New York: Cornell University Press, 1958), pp. 47–72; James V. Compton, *The Swastika and the Eagle* (Boston: Houghton Mifflin, 1967), pp. 161–73; and Saul Friedlander, *Prelude to Downfall: Hitler and the United States, 1939–1941* (New York: Knopf, 1967).

It is of course true that Germany, not the United States, ultimately made the Atlantic war overt. Four days after Pearl Harbor, Hitler declared war on America. He was not strictly required to do so by the terms of his alliance since Japan struck first. The alliance had always been considered as a deterrent to keep America out of the war by confronting her with a two-front conflict if she tried to deal with just one opponent at a time. Even the Tokyo War Crimes Tribunal accepted this explanation.

We probably never will understand this decision fully, rooted as it must have been in Hitler's psychopathology. But it does seem that by December 1941 Hitler had become convinced that conflict between himself and the United States, arising out of the Atlantic naval engagements, was imminent in any case. Under those circumstances he could not afford to lose the goodwill of Japan, and in fact for a long time hoped that the Japanese would reciprocate his gesture by turning also on the Russians.[6] Thus he took the step that sealed his downfall.

Had America remained in the status of twilight belligerence Germany probably would not have been defeated, though as I have argued above, neither could it have won. Probably World War II would have ended in some sort of draw and negotiated settlement, or would have continued on for a decade or two with occasional truces for breathing spells— not unlike the Napoleonic Wars. Or perhaps most likely is some combination of the two, in which the negotiated peace was uneasy and soon broken. What I imagine, then, is a very long and bloody war, longer and even more bloody than the one that really was fought, with protracted savage fighting in east and central Europe.

Just where the truce line would have been drawn no one can say, of course, but it might well have approximated the present border of the Soviet Union. The Russians might have

6. Hans L. Trefousse, *Germany and American Neutrality, 1939–1941* (New York: Bookman, 1951).

recovered all their original territory plus the gains of 1939 (from Poland, Rumania, and Finland, and the three Baltic states). Quite likely they could have controlled Bulgaria and Rumania, but the rest of East Central Europe probably would have been German or German satellites as it was in 1941 at the beginning of Operation Barbarossa. Again, the details are speculative, but matter little. I doubt that the Soviets would have had to yield more than this, and if anything stood a greater chance of driving the Germans still further back. But this hypothetical boundary marks to me the greatest plausible German advance, and so provides an outer limit to the argument I shall develop further below. In any case, my assumption is that this "settlement" could have been reached only after a mutually exhausting war that would have left the Russians even more battered than they were from their victory in 1945, and the Germans hardly better.

In the West, Britain was both impregnable to German invasion and too weak to invade the German-held continent by herself. The North African campaign was important, especially to British postwar colonial hopes, but by 1942 was not the sort of effort that could bring defeat to either side. The undersea war in the North Atlantic was more dangerous to the British, but Hitler was nevertheless trapped in it. If pursued too vigorously, it would bring the Americans into the war. And if American shipping was in large part left immune from attack, British supply lines could not really be cut. The British surface blockade of the continent might have been more effective, but a similar kind of war had not been enough against either Napoleon or the Kaiser, and certainly was not in reality enough by itself to bring Hitler down in 1945. So stalemate there too seems by far the most plausible outcome. Hitler had persistent notions of forming an Anglo-German "partnership."[7]

Perhaps the British, under Churchill, would not have signed a formal compromise peace, as they indeed had refused to do

7. Sallagar, *Road to Total War*, p. 66.

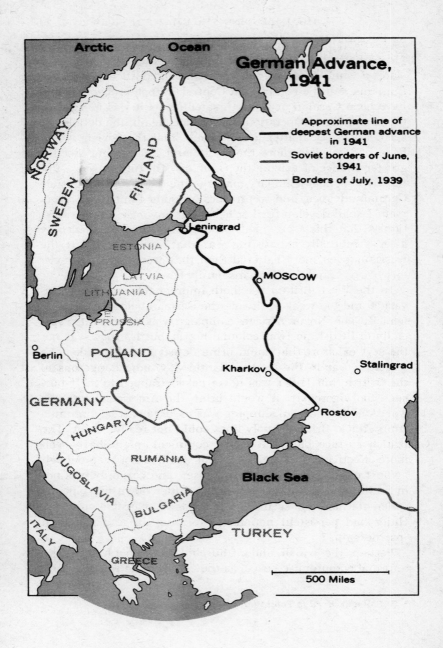

German Advance, 1941

Arctic Ocean

Approximate line of deepest German advance in 1941

Soviet borders of June, 1941

Borders of July, 1939

NORWAY

SWEDEN

FINLAND

ESTONIA

LATVIA

LITHUANIA

E. PRUSSIA

Leningrad

MOSCOW

Stalingrad

Kharkov

Berlin

POLAND

GERMANY

Rostov

HUNGARY

RUMANIA

YUGOSLAVIA

BULGARIA

Black Sea

ITALY

TURKEY

GREECE

500 Miles

in 1940 despite Hitler's apparent willingness. But in 1940 the British still could play for big stakes. They might lose, but also, if they could hold off the immediate German invasion, they had some very high cards with which to bid for ultimate victory. There was still the possibility of Russian entry on their side, and the United States remained to kindle memories of 1917. Later these cards would have lost their value, with a stalemate on the eastern front and, as we hypothesize, a determined American aloofness from actual entry into war. If Churchill would not have made the peace some other leader might have been given the chance. And even a deescalated but still belligerent stalemate would have had much the same effect from an American geopolitical viewpoint—the assumption of explicit negotiation and compromise is by no means necessary.

Under these conditions, Britain would have been left independent—economically weakened, and shorn of some colonies, but still a sovereign center of significant power. Russia would also have remained independent, probably with much the same boundaries as we now see (though no part of East Prussia, and fewer "satellites"), Germany would of course have emerged with enormously enhanced strength on the European continent, initially controlling essentially everything from Iberia to somewhere in the vicinity of Poland. (Sweden and Switzerland might either have been occupied or left cowed but independent; there is no way of knowing which.) The *upper limit* to the population of this empire would have been somewhere around 330 million—almost exactly the number currently in the Soviet orbit.

That population, nevertheless, would have been much more highly skilled than that of eastern Europe and equipped with greater physical capital; in principle it would have posed an appreciably greater ultimate threat to the rest of the world than would the same number of people under communist rule. Yet the situation in principle need not have been that way in fact. Some substantial proportion, perhaps as much as a quarter, would have been more directly under the control of Mussolini's Italy; while Rome and Berlin might have remained allied, it is hard to imagine perfect cooperation. Nationalism in general would surely have been as great a bane to Hitler as it has been to the Soviet Union. Ruling highly-educated and urbanized West and Central Europe would hardly have been easier for the Germans than a similar task has proven for the Russians. Particularly since Germans accounted for only about a quarter of the population of this area, in fact the task would probably have been still harder. George Kennan has pithily expressed this sentiment, relevant especially where the "master" nation is much in the minority, by quoting Gibbon: "There is nothing more contrary to nature than the attempt to hold in obedience distant provinces." Kennan applied this dictum to both German and Russian prospects for continental domination.[8]

Divisiveness, conflict, and schism have to be made part of any image of a German-dominated continent. So too must the need for reconstruction, after a devastating war with the Russians in much of the area and a draining blockade imposed by the British. It would have been quite a while before Hitler could have marshalled the resources of Europe for any serious further drive either east or west.

Contemporary alarms

Some contemporaries of course took a more alarmist view, especially immediately after the fall of France. A *Fortune* magazine survey of American in July 1940 found that 63 percent expected that an Axis triumph would bring an immediate German attempt to seize territory in the Western

8. George F. Kennan, *Memoirs, 1925–1950* (Boston: Little Brown, 1967, pp. 129–30. Kennan also argued, contrary to the widespread belief of the late 1940s, that Russia was not a serious military threat to the United States requiring rearmament or establishment of NATO. See Chapter 17 of *Memoirs*, and the section by Hammond in Warner Schilling, Paul Hammond and Glenn Snyder, *Strategy, Politics, and Defense Budgets* (New York: Columbia University Press, 1962).

Hemisphere; 43 percent expected an imminent attack on the United States.[9] American army generals feared a Nazi invasion of South America, and to forestall it wanted a major base in Trinidad.[10] The continued resistance of Britain calmed such alarm for a while, though it was to be revived in somewhat similar form in 1942 with the anticipation of German aerial attacks on American cities and towns. Seacoast areas were allotted major antiaircraft units. Blackout regulations were widely enforced. School children were taught how to crouch against basement walls clenching corks between their teeth in the event of bombardment. Fiorello LaGuardia, then head of the Office of Civilian Defense, wanted 50 million gas masks.[11]

All of this of course seems more than a little absurd in light of known—then as well as now—German capabilities. Not a single German bomb ever did fall in North or South America. Any kind of troop landing required naval and logistic support utterly beyond Hitler's reach. After all, it was not until two and a half years of war, with vast shipping and naval superiority, and a base in Britain, that the Allies felt able to cross even the English Channel in an invasion the other way. The bogeyman of Nazi troops in America had no more substance than that, several years later, of Russian landings.

This is not to say that ultimately a German victory might not have posed some such dangers, nor to imply any certainty about limitations to Hitler's intentions. A. J. P. Taylor paints Hitler as essentially a classical German statesman without real ambition to dominate Europe; Alan Bullock sees ambition, but directed largely toward Eastern Europe and certainly

9. Cited in Manfred Jonas, *Isolationism in America* (Ithaca, New York: Cornell University Press, 1966), p. 213.

10. Mark Skinner Watson, *Chief of Staff: Prewar Plans and Preparation* (Washington: Department of the Army, 1950).

11. Richard R. Lingeman, *Don't You Know There's a War On? The American Home Front, 1941–1945* (New York: G. P. Putnam's Sons, 1970), p. 36. In the winter of 1944–45 the commander of the Atlantic fleet ordered deactivated air raid wardens back to their posts, saying V–bomb attacks were not only "possible but probable," p. 267.

not toward the new world.[12] We need not accept either of these views. Other writers grant that the documents have turned up no German plan before December 1941 for a military attack on the United States, but contend that such plans might well have developed ultimately. One does show some Hitlerian ravings and notions of ultimate war with America, beginning in October 1940. This same author emphasizes that the mere absence of plans is no proof that Hitler did not have, or could not have developed, the intent.[13] At this point the argument of those who posit the possibility of a later threat becomes impossible to refute. One must ask realistic questions about German capability, not intention.

Very possibly a stalemate would not have marked the end of Hitler's ambitions, but that is not really the point. For some time at least, Germany would not have been supreme as an immediate menace to the United States. One further step in still another war would first be required—the ultimate victory over Britain and/or Russia, and if that should in fact be threatened, the United States could still have intervened *then*, and done so while allies existed. By the end of 1941 the pressure for such intervention had really passed for *that* war. Even those who most heavily stress the dangers of Nazi subversion in North and South America grant that "There still would be ominous eddies, but by the summer of 1940 the Nazi cause was in retreat in the new world."[14]

Two important "might have been" qualifications need to be acknowledged before one can be at all satisfied that the strategic scenario I have sketched is sufficiently plausible. The

12. A. J. P. Taylor, *The Origins of the Second World War* (New York: Atheneum, 1966); Alan Bullock, *Hitler: A Study in Tyranny* (New York: Harper and Row, 1962, rev. ed.).

13. Alton Frye, *Nazi Germany and the American Hemisphere, 1933–1941* (New Haven: Yale University Press, 1967), and Compton, *Swastika and the Eagle*.

14. Frye, *Nazi Germany*, p. 130. Hitler's psychic ability to pursue his grandiose aims successfully is also in doubt. One historian concludes, "Throughout his life, Adolf Hitler flirted with failure and involved himself unnecessarily in situations that were frought with danger." R. G. L. Waite, "Adolf Hitler's Guilt Feelings: A Problem in History and Psychology," *Journal of Interdisciplinary History* 1, no. 2 (1971): 239.

first is the possibility of a separate peace on the eastern front, another Hitler-Stalin pact, more durable and more dangerous than the one of August 1939. Certainly both leaders were unscrupulous and firmly in control of their governments; the possibility cannot be dismissed. But what kind of an agreement? Simply to call off the war and accept a compromise settlement? That in fact is what we have hypothesized in the above scenario, no different except that possibly the agreement could have come "too soon" before both were sufficiently bled to cut into their power to threaten others.

An agreement to become cobelligerents against the British, with Stalin changing sides, does seem implausible. For strategic reasons if for no others, Germany was a far greater threat to Russia than was Britain. Britain, with a navy but only a small army, was far distant from the great and nearly self-sufficient Russian land-mass; Germany, with a great army, was Russia's neighbor. Once they had drawn each others' blood to the extent they had in the first six months of war, could they conceivably have trusted each other sufficiently in a negotiated peace for the Germans to turn their forces westward? So long as the Nazi political and military machines were intact, could the Russians have undertaken serious ventures that would reduce their screening forces against another German attack? Given the mental states of the two dictators, could they really have maintained a stable alliance relationship for very long? Stalin was paranoid enough not to trust anyone, certainly not Hitler. But he would have had to be a raving maniac actively to help Hitler bring down Germany's last opponent.

The Bomb

The other potential flaw is The Bomb. Lacking the immense pressures of actual participation in World War II, the United States might not have pressed its nuclear research program so hard. Without question fewer resources would have been put into the Manhattan project, and explosion of the first bomb delayed. Might it have been postponed long enough for Germany to get its own bomb first, and in sufficient quantity to tip the military balance from stalemate? The possibility cannot be dismissed, but it does not appear to be a strong one. The American nuclear effort received its first military money in 1940, and already had made important progress before Pearl Harbor. Though delayed, achievement of a bomb in America probably would have occurred by 1946 or 1947. As was discovered by their somewhat surprised conquerors in 1945, the Germans were not at all close to getting their own bomb; the western allies had feared they were farther along than they proved to be.

> There seems never to have been formulated a feasible plan for producing any fission device that could be expected to aid in bringing a German victory . . . Until the very last we could hardly believe that the Germans' fission studies were achieving nothing of military significance.[15]

Furthermore, there are very few examples in modern warfare between industrial nations where one state achieves a decisive military advantage over the other with a new weapon. Even given military secrecy, weapons *development* is dependent upon a *scientific* base that is international and largely a matter of public information. Hence, any large industrial state has access to this base for military applications. And since the stages of procurement and installation normally take so long even after a weapon is developed, an initially laggard state has a good bit of time to catch up before the other has the weapon in sufficient quantity to change the military balance critically. Certainly during World War I none of the major innovations, such as tanks or gas, gave a

15. Arthur H. Compton, *Atomic Quest: A Personal Narrative* (New York: Oxford University Press, 1956), p. 225. See also Speer, *Inside*, pp. 225–29.

decisive advantage to either side, although if procured secretly in great quantity and then unleashed they did have that potential. Nor was the actual use of atomic bombs in 1945 such a deviation from the above principle as it may seem. The United States had only two bombs in August 1945, and used both.[16] They were enough to induce surrender (but just barely) by an already beaten opponent, but could not have had that effect against an economically and militarily still viable state.

Thus: 1) Even without the great pressures of actual participation in World War II, the United States (or Britain) might very well have developed the atomic bomb before Germany did anyway. This of course assumes that the United States was truly carrying on a major program of rearmament and preparedness, perhaps equivalent to the eight-to-ten percent of gross national product (GNP) spent on defense that has been typical of the last two decades. But the whole discussion, not just the point about the atom bomb, depends on this assumption. 2) Should the Germans have made the bomb first, they were unlikely to do so with sufficient lead time over the Americans and British to procure bombs in a quantity that could determine the outcome of the war. Delivery vehicles would have constituted an additional problem to the Germans. In 1945 they were still possibly as much as a decade away from a capability of bombing the United States effectively. (The same was proved true of the Russians.) One must admit that the tight little islands of the British were most vulnerable, and there is a chance, small but real, that German atom bombs, perhaps delivered by V-weapons, could have been critical there. But perhaps the strongest caution against exaggerating the effect of a possible German bomb comes from recalling how little confidence many American governmental officials later had in the military utility of

16. A third was being completed, but was not ready until after the Japanese capitulation. Richard C. Hewlett and Oscar E. Anderson, *The New World, 1939/1946* (University Park: Pennsylvania State University Press, 1962), p. 405.

their own bomb. For several years after World War II, and despite the American nuclear monopoly, they feared they could not deter Russia from military adventures.

If we do acknowledge some possibility that American aloofness from combat *could*, despite my arguments, have led to a very bad outcome, a clear-cut German victory, we should also acknowledge the perhaps equal chance that the Nazis might have been soundly defeated by the British and Russians alone. After long years of economic blockade and slowly-building Soviet strength, ultimate German defeat is not utterly implausible. Maybe Britain, with Canadian help, would have gotten the bomb first. Also, it is quite conceivable that Hitler would have been overthrown. The July 1944 attempt on his life was, after all, a very close thing, a matter of a couple of feet in the placement of the briefcase bomb under his table. A long, wearing war going beyond spring 1945 would undoubtedly have generated new pressures for his removal.

Two aspects of this argument should nevertheless be made clear. First, some of it is being made with all the advantages of hindsight; while the general outline might have been clear to Franklin Roosevelt at the end of 1941, it may be unfair to expect, retrospectively, that he should have foreseen the stalemate outcome. Perhaps the most important component in the stalemate thesis is the German defeat at Stalingrad, and no one could have *relied* upon that. A no-win solution should have appeared as a very possible ending to the war, but with the incomplete returns before Pearl Harbor, depending on it would have seemed to pose great risks. (On the other hand, no political figure at that time really foresaw the chance that Germany might develop atomic weapons, which becomes a hindsight argument in justification of intervention.) The most important flaw that one can find in Roosevelt's policy is one for which he has been often and roundly denounced—the failure to comprehend how unavoidably American intervention, if successful, would bring Russia into Central Europe to fill the vacuum left by defeated Germany. The demand for unconditional surrender was to make this inescapable.

Even less does this argument imply criticism of Winston Churchill's basic policy. For the United States, the continued independence of Britain was to provide the margin, the buffer, to make nonintervention an acceptable strategy. As long as Britain was there, to serve as an ally and absorb the initial impact of any German attack in a later round, conceding a compromise peace to Hitler raised only tolerable risks. The United States was distant, possessed great resources for a mobilization base, and would not be immediately harmed in any serious way by German domination of much of the continent. But Britain had none of these luxuries. Even should one accept A. J. P. Taylor's view of Hitler's intentions, the consequences of new German strength carried great risk. Utter destruction of the traditional European balance of power and German presence on the other side of the Straits of Dover would be too much to bear. Britain would then be in the front lines, and she had to fight for a peace that would leave her a greater margin. For Britain, equivalent resources in Russian hands almost a thousand miles away would pose a little less threat than in possession of the more proximate Germans.

A moral imperative?

Finally, we ought to confront the argument that sheer morality demanded American intervention against Hitler. I have deliberately left this issue aside, defining our concern to be only with the structure of the international system, the relative weight of power facing the United States and its potential allies. My argument has accepted the "realist" one that fears the concentration of great power in other hands regardless of the apparent goals, ideology, or morality of those wielding that power. Concern with the morality of others' domestic politics is an expensive luxury, and evaluations all too subject to rapid change. (Consider, for example, the wobbly course of many Americans' attitudes toward the government of Chiang Kai-shek.) By this view one should be indifferent between Stalin and Hitler except as one of them possessed greater power.

Yet some would maintain that Hitler was just too evil to tolerate, that the United States had a moral duty to exterminate him and free those under his rule. Without question to most of us, Hitler was indeed a very evil man. His murder of approximately ten million civilians (in addition to the six million Jews there were others: Poles, Gypsies, and other alleged *untermenschen*) can hardly be ignored, and I do not doubt that he would have been capable of even greater atrocities had he lived longer and ruled a wider area.

Still, in this context Hitler must be compared with Stalin, who was hardly a saint, and who as a result of the complete German collapse in 1945 emerged from the war with an immensely greater empire. We must remember the terror and paranoid purges of his rule, and such examples of Stalinist humanity as the starvation of millions of kulaks. The worst Nazi crimes emerged only in 1943 and later at Nuremberg. German "medical experiments" and extermination camps were unknown to the world in 1941. Though the Hitler regime had anything but a savory reputation then, the moral argument too is essentially one made in hindsight, not a primary motivation at the time war was declared. Nor in fact did the war save very many Jews. Hardly more than 20 percent of European Jewish population alive at the time of Pearl Harbor survived at the end.[17] War-time opportunities to bargain with the Nazis for Jewish lives were ignored.

I personally find it hard to develop a very emphatic preference for Stalinist Russia over Hitlerite Germany, but *chacun à son gout*. In cold-blooded realist terms, Nazism as an ideology was almost certainly less dangerous to the United States than is Communism. Marxism-Leninism has a worldwide ap-

17. According to Raul Hilberg, *The Destruction of the European Jews* (Chicago: Quadrangle, 1961), p. 767, approximately 970,000 survived in Eastern Europe outside the Soviet Union. Perhaps another 700,000 on the continent of Western Europe were spared.

peal; Nazism lacks much palatability to non-Aryan tastes. But if in the end one wants to argue that the horrors of Nazism were too great and so warranted American intervention, that is a perfectly reasonable position *so long as one states it clearly.* A powerful argument may be that in Western Europe—France, the Low Countries, Scandinavia, Italy, and Germany itself—stalemate under Nazi occupation would have meant social transformations that might have doomed for many years the culture of parliamentary democracy. It could be rescued by American intervention (as Eastern Europe could not) providing that the intervention came soon. While the survival of democracy on the continent was not central to American strategic or material interests, many of us, this author included, would deplore its loss. At the same time, a purely moral basis for war must not be confused with the objective threat to American national security that Germany did or did not constitute.

3

A Hobson's Choice
for Japan

Japan in China

If one rejects the purely moral justification of American entry into the war against Hitler, no very effective moral brief can then be made for the war in the Pacific. True, the Japanese were often unkind conquerors, though this can easily be exaggerated by American memories of the Bataan death march and other horrors in the treatment of prisoners. Japanese occupation was often welcomed in the former European colonies of Southeast Asia, and Japan retains some reservoir of good will for its assistance, late in the war, of indigenous liberation movements. In any case it is Hitler, not Tojo, who is customarily presented as the personification of evil. Possibly Americans did have some vague obligation to defend Chinese independence, but more clearly than in Europe the basis for American participation has to be *realpolitik*. The case has to be founded on a conviction that Japan was too powerful, too dangerously expansionist without any apparent restraint, to have been left alone. An extreme but widely accepted version is given by an early chronicler of the war:

> Japan in the spring and summer of 1941 would accept no diplomatic arrangement which did not give it every-

thing that it might win in the Far East by aggression, without the trouble and expense of military campaigns.[1]

The evidence, however, shows quite a different picture both of intent and capability. Nor is it enough simply to assert that, because Japan attacked the United States at Pearl Harbor, America took no action to begin hostilities. This is formally true, but very deceptive. The Japanese attack would not have come but for the American, British, and Dutch embargo on shipment of strategic raw materials to Japan. Japan's strike against the American naval base merely climaxed a long series of mutually antagonistic acts. In initiating economic sanctions against Japan the United States undertook actions that were widely recognized in Washington as carrying grave risk of war. To understand this requires a retracing of the events of the preceding years.

By the beginning of the 1940s Japan was involved in an exhausting and seemingly endless war on the Asian mainland. The "China incident" dated back to the Japanese seizure of Manchuria in 1931, and was greatly escalated by the clash at the Marco Polo Bridge which expanded into severe open warfare with China in 1937. Although the Army did willfully create an incident at Mukden in 1931, the Marco Polo Bridge affair seems not to have been a deliberate provocation by Tokyo. Nevertheless most Japanese military and political leaders did seek a "Co-Prosperity Sphere" of economic and political predominance. They apparently believed that their Empire's status as an independent world power depended on military equality with Russia and the United States in the Far East; that in turn depended on a hegemonial position, preferably economic but achieved by force if necessary, in the

1. Basil Rauch, *Roosevelt, from Munich to Pearl Harbor* (New York: Creative Age Press, 1950), p. 396.

area of China.[2] Though this seems strange now, an adequate view of Japanese policy in its contemporary context has to remember Tokyo's position as a latecomer to colonialism, in a world where France, Britain, and the United States all had their own spheres of influence.

Japanese forces made important initial gains by occupying most of the Chinese coast and most of China's industrial capacity, but with a trickle of American aid the nationalist armies hung on in the interior. By 1941 the Japanese armies were bogged down, and their progress greatly impeded by raw material shortages. In 1940 Congress placed fuel oil and scrap iron under the new National Defense Act as goods which could not be shipped out of the Western Hemisphere without an export license. Although commerce in these products was not actually cut off for another year, the threat to Japan of a raw material scarcity was obvious, and deliberately invoked by an American government seeking to apply pressure against the Japanese campaign in China. This strategy was exercised in a series of dozens of gradually tightening economic measures—an escalation that was to drive Japan not to capitulation, as it was intended to do, but to war with the United States.[3]

Following the July 1941 freeze on Japanese assets in America, and the consequent cessation of shipment of oil, scrap iron, and other goods from the United States, Japan's economy was in most severe straits and her power to wage war directly threatened. Her military leaders estimated that her reserves of oil, painfully accumulated in the late 1930s when the risk of just such a squeeze became evident, would last at most two years. She was also short of rice, tin, bauxite, nickel, rubber and other raw materials normally imported from the Dutch East Indies and Malaya. Negotiations with the Dutch

2. James B. Crowley, *Japan's Quest for Autonomy: National Security and Foreign Policy, 1930–1938* (Princeton: Princeton University Press, 1966).

3. On the slow, very deliberate application of economic sanctions see John Morton Blum, *From the Morgenthau Diaries: Years of Urgency, 1938–1941* (Boston: Houghton Mifflin, 1965), Chapter 10.

authorities to supply these goods, plus extraordinary amounts of oil from the wells of Sumatra, had failed, ostensibly on the grounds that the Dutch feared the material would be reexported to the Axis in Europe. The United States, and the British and Dutch, made it quite clear that the embargo would be relaxed only in exchange for Japanese withdrawal from air and naval bases in Indochina (seized in order to prosecute better the war against China) and an agreement which would have meant the end of the Japanese involvement in China and the *abandonment* of any right to station troops in that country, not just a halt to the fighting. The purpose of the Western economic blockade was to force a favorable solution to the "China incident."

Under these conditions, the High Command of the Japanese navy demanded a "settlement" of one sort or other that would restore Japan's access to essential raw materials, most particularly oil. Without restored imports of fuel the fleet could not very long remain an effective fighting force. While the navy might have been willing to abandon the China campaign, it was utterly opposed to indefinite continuation of the status quo. Either raw material supplies had to be restored by a peaceful settlement with the Western powers, or access to the resources in Thailand, Malaya, and the Indies would have to be secured by force while Japan still retained the capabilities to do so.

If the navy demanded either settlement or war, most members of the Japanese elite were opposed to any settlement which would in effect have meant withdrawal from China. No serious thought was given to the possibility of peace with Chiang's government, for it would have meant the end of all hopes of empire in East Asia and even, it was thought, of influence on the continent of Asia. Moderate Foreign Minister Shigenori Togo reacted to the most forceful statement of American demands, on November 27, 1941, "Japan was asked not only to abandon all the gains of her years of sacrifice, but to surrender her international position as a power in the Far

East." In his view, that surrender would have been equivalent to national suicide.[4]

In any case, the Army High Command simply would not have tolerated any abandonment of its position in China. Its own prestige and influence had been built up step by step during the war there, and its position in China became its power base in Japanese domestic politics. General Hideki Tojo, by no means the most violent of the Army war hawks, feared that any concession on the China issue would risk an actual revolt by extremist elements in the Army. In fact, on the resignation of Prince Konoye's government in October 1941 Tojo had urged the appointment of Prince Higashi-Kuni as Premier, on the principle that, should a compromise with the United States be decided upon, only a member of the royal family would have a chance to control the Army and make peace. In the context of Japanese politics of the 1930s, when there had been several plotted coups and when one after another of the political leaders thought to be too conciliatory toward foreign elements were assassinated by extreme nationalists, this was hardly a far-fetched fear. Togo once characterized the Japanese internal political situation in these terms to Joseph C. Grew, American Ambassador to Tokyo, "If Japan were forced to give up suddenly all the fruits of the long war in China, collapse would follow."[5] Before we judge the Japanese too harshly Americans must remember their own difficulties in terminating a stalemated war 30 years later.

    4. Quoted in Herbert Feis, *The Road to Pearl Harbor* (Princeton: Princeton University Press, 1950), p. 327.
    5. See David J. Lu, *From the Marco Polo Bridge to Pearl Harbor: Japan's Entry into World War II* (Washington: Public Affairs Press, 1961), p. 304. See also the statement of the Japanese minister of war at the cabinet meeting of October 12, 1941: "The problem of the stationing of the troops in China in itself means the life of the Army, and we shall not be able to make any concessions at all." Quoted in the memoirs of Prince Konoye. U.S. Congress, Joint Committee on the Investigation of Pearl Harbor Attack, *Pearl Harbor Attack: Hearings Before the Joint Committee*, 79th Congress, 1st Session (Washington: U.S. Government Printing Office, 1946), Part 20, p. 4009.

The hardening American commitment

Thus, for the various elements in the Japanese government, and for somewhat different reasons, a peaceful settlement ultimately become unacceptable. They could not accede to the American demands, and they could not even continue to drag out the negotiations because of the increasingly precarious nature of the war economy and especially the Navy's fuel supplies. On rejecting this unpalatable alternative they were again thrown back on the other; the necessary raw material could be obtained only by seizing Thailand, where there was rice; Malaya, with its sources of tin, nickel, and rubber; and the Dutch East Indies, with their oil. But, according to the Japanese calculations, the United States was certain to fight if British or Dutch territory in the Far East were attacked. Japanese analysts reached the latter conclusion despite the absence of any American threat or promise. At the Atlantic Conference, Roosevelt had acceded to Churchill's plea that he issue a "war warning" with regard to any further conquests by Japan in the Far East. After he returned to Washington, however, the State Department dissuaded him and no such warning was ever issued. The nearest equivalents were two statements by President Roosevelt to Ambassador Nomura in July and August of 1941. The first declared:

> If Japan attempted to seize oil supplies by force in the Netherlands East Indies, the Dutch would, without the shadow of doubt, resist, the British would immediately come to their assistance, and, in view of our policy of assisting Great Britain, an exceedingly serious situation would immediately result.[6]

6. Quoted in Langer and Gleason, *Undeclared War,* p. 650.

On the second occasion Roosevelt stated:

> If the Japanese Government takes any further steps in
> pursuance of a policy of program of military domination
> by force or threat of force of neighboring countries the
> government of the United States will be compelled to
> take immediately any and all steps which it may deem
> necessary toward safeguarding the legitimate rights and
> interests of the United States and American nationals
> and toward insuring the safety and security of the United
> States.[7]

Despite its firm language, this was not an unequivocal
warning. On presentation to Nomura it was, as Langer and
Gleason point out, not given the status of a "written statement" or even of an "oral statement." It was merely private
"reference material," for Nomura's use in communicating
with his own government. No unequivocal warning could be
given, simply because President Roosevelt could not be sure
of American reaction in the actual event of crisis. He was
fully aware of the need to secure congressional approval for
war, of the strength of isolationist sentiment in the United
States, of the difficulties involved in demonstrating that an
attack on British and Dutch colonies was a direct threat to
American interests, and of the dangers inherent in going to
war with the country deeply divided.

By autumn 1941, however, opinion was crystalizing in the
highest levels of the American decision-making system. In
November, Roosevelt informally polled his cabinet on the
question of whether the country would support war against
Japan in the event of attack on Malaya or the Indies. All
members responded in the affirmative. General Marshall and
Admiral Stark, the Chiefs of Staff, concluded that the United
States should fight if Japan attacked British or Dutch terri-

7. Ibid., p. 695. On the contrast between these and the agreement
with Churchill see Theodore A. Wilson, *The First Summit: Roosevelt
and Churchill at Placentia Bay, 1941* (Boston: Houghton Mifflin, 1969).

tory, or Siam west of 100 degrees East or south of 10 degrees North. In two conversations on December 1 and 3 Roosevelt assured Lord Halifax, British Ambassador to Washington, that the United States would give Britain armed support if the Japanese attacked British or Dutch territories, or if Britain went to war as a result of a Japanese landing in Siam. This assurance was communicated to London, and from there to Sir Robert Brooke-Popham, British commander in the Far East.[8] On the morning of December 7 in Washington (before the Pearl Harbor raid, which took place at dawn, Hawaii time) Secretaries Hull (State), Knox (Navy), and Stimson (War) discussed the anticipated Japanese attack on Siam or Malaya. They agreed the United States should go to war if the British did. Roosevelt then expected to go before Congress the next day to explain why a Japanese invasion of Siam threatened the security of the United States.

These decisions came too late, however, to affect directly the Japanese deliberations. By the beginning of December their attack was irrevocably set in motion. The Japanese conviction that war could not be limited to the British and Dutch had to be based wholly on inference. Yet it was a correct analysis and a solid conviction, as shown by the otherwise inexplicable risk they took at Pearl Harbor.

The perception of encirclement

Rather close links had been forged between the United States and the colonies in Malaya and the East Indies, bonds that were known to the Japanese and considered to be of great importance. The Southwest Pacific area was of undeniable economic importance to the United States—at the time most

8. Raymond A. Esthus, "President Roosevelt's Commitment to Intervene in a Pacific War," *Mississippi Valley Historical Review* 50, no. 1 (June 1963): 34.

of America's tin and rubber came from there, as did substantial quantities of other raw materials.[9] American political involvement in the area was also heavy. The United States was cooperating closely with the British and Dutch governments, and according to the Japanese evaluation, if the United States failed to defend the Indies it would lose its influence in China and endanger the Philippines.[10] Premier Tojo even referred in this context to the approval given Pan American World Airways to establish an air route between Singapore and Manila.[11]

Unilateral American actions to build up their military forces, both generally and in the Pacific in particular, were seen as evidence of aggressive intent.[12] But most convincing of all were the military ties apparently being established among the ABCD (American-British-Chinese-Dutch) powers. The United States was known to be supplying munitions and arms, including aircraft, not just to China but to British and Dutch forces in the Pacific. In cooperation with the British, Dutch, Australians, New Zealanders, and the Free French (at New Caledonia), the United States had begun construction of a string of airfields to the Philippines. Furthermore, the United States had participated in staff conversations with British and Dutch military personnel at Singapore. The Japanese came to associate these conversations with an "Anglo-American policy of encirclement against Japan in the South-

9. The economic importance of the area to the United States was not left to Japanese imagination. On July 11, 1940 Ambassador Grew pointed out to foreign minister Arita that in 1937 15.8 percent of the foreign trade of the Netherlands East Indies had been with the United States, and only 11.6 per cent with Japan. He further emphasized the interest of the United States in continuance of the open door there. See Cordell Hull, *The Memoirs of Cordell Hull*, Vol. I (New York: Macmillan, 1948), pp. 895–96.

10. See the Japanese Foreign Office memorandum of early November 1941, International Military Tribunal for the Far East (hereafter cited as IMTFE), *Document No. 1559A*. Similar conclusions were expressed in the Liaison Conference Meetings of October 1941, according to Robert J. C. Butow, *Tojo and the Coming of the War* (Princeton: Princeton University Press, 1961), p. 317–18.

11. Butow, *Tojo*, p. 225.

12. IMTFE, *Transcript of Proceedings*, p. 36246.

ern Pacific Ocean."[13] This notion of encirclement appears time and again in Japanese official documents and memoirs. The freezing of Japanese assets by the United States, British, and Netherlands East Indies governments occurred on the same day: July 26, 1941. Although that act was in direct response to Japan's occupation of southern Indo-China, her leaders nevertheless saw it as the final link in their bondage.[14]

As early as spring 1941, in fact, the Japanese army and navy general staffs had agreed among themselves that military action in the Southwest Pacific meant war with the United States. As we have seen, no definite decision by the United States had been reached, due largely to the state of American public opinion. But President Roosevelt and Secretary Hull were quite willing to have the Japanese believe that a joint American-British-Dutch plan of defense of the Indies existed.[15] The conviction only grew stronger with time, and was reinforced by the intelligence received from the Japanese embassy in Washington. On December 3, 1941, for example, the Washington embassy cabled Tokyo: "Judging from all indications, we feel that some joint military action between Great Britain and the United States, with or without a declaration of war, is a definite certainty in the event of an occupation of Thailand."[16]

The American fleet in the Pacific, while inferior to the Japanese in many respects, was strong enough to endanger seriously a sustained offensive and quite possibly strong enough to postpone Japan's effective occupation of the Indies

13. See the Foreign Office memorandum so entitled, July 1941, IMTFE: *Defense Document No. 1982*. Foreign Minister Shigenori Togo in his memoirs, *The Cause of Japan* (New York: Simon and Schuster, 1956), pp. 84, 156, 163, repeatedly referred to the conversations this way.
14. IMTFE, *Transcript*, p. 36273.
15. Feis, *Road to Pearl Harbor*, p. 190.
16. Quoted in U.S. Congress, Joint Committee on the Investigation of the Pearl Harbor Attack, *Investigation of Pearl Harbor Attack: Report of the Joint Committee*, 79th Congress, 2nd Session (Washington: U.S. Government Printing Office, 1946), p. 172. See also Nobutaka Ike, ed., *Japan's Decision for War: Records of the 1941 Policy Conferences* (Stanford: Stanford University Press, 1967), p. 350.

until her raw materials ran out. The oil fields might be put
out of operation for many months, and in any case the shipment of these supplies to Japan under the threat of American
air and naval attack would be too risky. Japan simply dared
not undertake such operations while the American fleet remained intact.

Having decided against withdrawal from China, failed to
negotiate a settlement with America, and decided on the
necessity of seizing supplies from Southeast Asia, they were
faced with the need to blunt what they regarded as the inevitable American response. Thus they launched a surprise
attack on Pearl Harbor to destroy any American capability for
immediate naval offensive. For all the audacity of the strike
at Hawaii, its aims were limited: to destroy existing United
States offensive capabilities in the Pacific by tactical surprise.
The Japanese High Command hoped only to give its forces
time to occupy the islands of the Southwest Pacific, to extract
those islands' raw materials, and to turn the whole area into
a virtually impregnable line of defense which could long de-
lay an American counteroffensive and mete out heavy casualties when the counterattack did come. As a result of their
early success the Japanese naval and military chiefs extended
this line a little farther than they had first meant to do, but
their original intentions were not grandiose.

In deciding to attack Pearl Harbor the Japanese took what
they fully recognized to be a great risk. There is no doubt but
that the Imperial government realized it could not win a long
war with the United States if the Americans chose to fight
such a war. Japanese strategists calculated that America's
war potential was seven to eight times greater than their own;
they knew that Japan could not hope to carry the war to the
continental United States. General Suzuki, chairman of the
Planning Board, had reported that Japan's stockpile of resources was not adequate to support a long war. Admiral
Yamamoto, the brilliant inventor of the Pearl Harbor attack
plan, warned: "In the first six months to a year of war against
the U.S. and England I will run wild, and I will show you an

uninterrupted succession of victories; I must also tell you that, should the war be prolonged for two or three years, I have no confidence in our ultimate victory."[17]

Because the proposed attack seemed an escape from the dilemma it was grasped with more enthusiasm than it deserved. The Japanese never seriously considered exactly what would cause the United States to forego crushing Japan, or how Japan might best create the proper conditions for a negotiated peace. Certain key elements, such as the probable effect of the Pearl Harbor attack on the American will to win, were left completely unanalyzed. Japan's sole strategy involved dealing maximum losses to the United States at the outset, making the prospects of a prolonged war as grim as possible, and counting, in an extremely vague and ill-defined way, on the American people's "softness" to end the war.

A considered decision

Nor, certainly, can the Japanese decision be explained simply as an act of "irrationality," an impulsive act by an unstable leader. Such explanations depend either upon a situation of great stress, which would warp the actions of all or most of the participants in the decision process, or really apply only to circumstances where a single individual in fact makes the decision. Some of Hitler's most costly mistakes in World War II, for example, were highly individualistic decisions for which he alone was responsible. Typical of the pattern was his order to stand and fight at Stalingrad rather than allow his army to retreat and regroup. High stress plus the peculiarities of the Fuehrer's personality produced a command different from what other men would have given.

The Japanese decision to attack Pearl Harbor, however,

17. Quoted in Roberta Wohlstetter, *Pearl Harbor: Warning and Decision* (Stanford: Stanford University Press, 1962), p. 350.

was neither the decision of a single individual, where much of his behavior could be explained by his own personality, nor a decision arrived at under time pressures. It was reached incrementally and reinforced at several steps along the line. On July 2, 1941, it was decided to press ahead with expansion in Southeast Asia even though this meant a high risk of war with the United States. After deep consideration by high Japanese military and naval officials for months, a formal commitment was made at the Imperial Conference of September 6 that either negotiations must result in lifting the United States embargo on strategic raw materials, or Japan would have to fight the Americans. October 15 was set as the deadline for success in negotiation. But even though the strategic commitment (in the sense of a decision for the next move dependent upon the opponent's reaction to this one) had seemingly been made, it was the subject of a great deal of reexamination over the subsequent three months. Prince Konoye's government resigned following the expiration of the deadline, but the new cabinet formed under General Tojo took office not as a regime determined to take the nation into war, but rather as one still seeking a way out. Serious negotiation with the United States continued through November. A new secret deadline of November 25 was once set, "after which things are going to happen automatically," but it too was extended until November 30.

Whatever the nature of the decision to go to war, it was arrived at and reinforced over a long period of time, and was not the result of anyone's possibly "irrational" impulse. In any case, the decision was in no important sense the act of a single man whose peculiar traits can be used to explain it. Rather, it was a carefully—if incompletely—considered collective attempt to break out of a dilemma that no man would relish.

This analysis is meant to establish an important proposition: that the Japanese attack on Pearl Harbor, and for that matter on Southeast Asia, is not evidence of any unlimited expansionist policy or capability by the Japanese government.

It was the consequence only of a much less ambitious goal, centering on an unwillingness to surrender the position that the Japanese had fought for years to establish in China. When that refusal met an equal American determination that Japan should give up many of her gains in China, the result was war. Japanese expansion into Southeast Asia originated less in strength than in weakness; it was predominantly instrumental to the China campaign, not a reach for another slice of global salami. Of course there were Japanese political and military leaders with wider ambitions, but they were not predominant in policy-making.

Throughout the 1930s the United States government had done little to resist the Japanese advance on the Asian continent. There were verbal protests, but little more. Even in early 1941 Washington apparently would have settled for a *halt* in China, and saw little danger of a much wider move into Southeast Asia. But the application of economic sanctions against Tokyo was very successful; it was obviously hurting, and the moderate Premier Prince Konoye proposed a direct meeting with Roosevelt to try to reach an understanding. At about that point the American Government seems to have been so impressed with its success that it rebuffed Konoye's approach, demanding that he agree in advance on terms of a settlement. Konoye's cabinet fell, and American observers concluded—on the basis of untestable evidence that sounded a bit like sour grapes—that he could not have enforced a "reasonable" settlement in Japanese politics anyway. Washington then raised the ante, calling for a Japanese *withdrawal* from all occupied territory in China. Several officials in the State Department proposed settling for a halt, giving China a breathing spell that would have served it better for several more years of war while America made its main effort in the Atlantic. Hull considered and then rejected their plan for such a *modus vivendi*, which rather closely resembled the second of two Japanese proposals ("Plan B") that represented Tokyo's last efforts. Economic sanctions continued to provide a warm moral glow for those who disapproved of trading with an aggressor, but they then served to make inevitable an otherwise avoidable war which was peripheral to American vital interests and for which the country was ill-prepared.

It was widely understood in Washington that the next move would probably be some sort of Japanese attack in Southeast Asia. Ambassador Grew in Tokyo had long been warning of the limited nature of Japanese goals and the consequences of resisting them.[18] As early as 1940, Under-secretary of State Sumner Welles had cautioned that an embargo would bring Japanese occupation of the Dutch East Indies.

America in China

Why then did President Roosevelt and his advisers embark on a series of incremental pressures that had the effect of pushing the Japanese into war? In large part, of course, they decided that Japanese ambitions in China posed a long-term threat to American interests, and so they forced a confrontation. A sentimental American attitude toward China as a "ward" also must not be forgotten. From missionary days they had been a people "we had always helped," to whom there was a sense of obligation.[19] Roosevelt had a long-time emotional attachment to China, and from his days as Assistant Secretary of the Navy had allegedly "become imbued

18. See Schroeder, *Axis Alliance,* esp. pp. 168–82, and on the earlier period Dorothy Borg, *The United States and the Far Eastern Crisis of 1933–1938* (Cambridge: Harvard University Press, 1964). Grew's warnings are related in his *Turbulent Era: A Diplomatic Record of Forty Years, 1904–1945* (Boston: Houghton-Mifflin, 1952).

19. For a penetrating documentation of these and other superficial attitudes by "representative examples of American leadership types" see Harold R. Isaacs, *Scratches on Our Minds: American Images of China and India* (New York: John Day, 1958). See also John K. Fairbank, *The United States and China* (Cambridge: Harvard University Press, 1959), rev. ed., Chapter 14.

with the Navy's conviction that Japan was America's Number One enemy."[20]

Nor should economic, as opposed to strategic, motives be ignored as they have been in most conventional histories of the period. Beginning with Dr. Sun Yat-Sen's idea that Chinese reconstruction would have to be brought about in collaboration with other countries, the nationalist government sought foreign economic and technical assistance.[21] Some interest was expressed in the United States, with a few loans forthcoming. Nondiscrimination in East Asian trade was almost always included in American demands on Japan. According to one analyst with a revisionist perspective

Although the Great China Market never materialized, many American leaders in the New Deal period . . . acted upon the assumption that it would, and this gave them reason to oppose Japan's forward movement in Asia.[22]

Another demonstrates the importance of perceived commercial possibilities in China in the first American extension of economic assistance to belligerent China.[23] Yet another, commenting on policy toward all the Axis states, says:

The actual defense of the United States was one factor involved in the move to an "all-out aid short of war" policy, but the restoration of the Open Door world order was of at least equal importance to the Roosevelt administration.[24]

20. Sumner Welles, *Seven Decisions that Shaped the World* (New York: Harper and Row, 1951), p. 68.
21. Borg, *Far Eastern Crisis*, p. 56.
22. Lloyd C. Gardner, *Economic Aspects of New Deal Diplomacy* (Madison: University of Wisconsin Press, 1964), p. 328.
23. Frederick C. Adams, "The Road to Pearl Harbor: A Reexamination of American Far Eastern Policy, July 1937–December 1938," *Journal of American History* 58, no. 1 (June 1971): 73–92.
24. Robert F. Smith, "American Foreign Relations, 1920–1942," in Barton J. Bernstein, ed., *Towards a New Past: Dissenting Essays in American History* (New York: Pantheon, 1968), p. 251.

Such considerations surely applied, and probably in greater strength, to continental Europe, where Nazi plans for autarchy threatened an American market that was quantitatively very much more important.[25] The economic prospect of a German-Soviet dominated Europe must have seemed unattractive—though, objectively, the threat to the national interest as a whole amounted to less than two percent of American GNP for those exports and imports combined. There also was some fear of German economic penetration into South America. But as for the Far East, by embargoing Japan in 1941 the United States was giving up an export trade at least four times that with China. While one must not equate dollar volume perfectly with relative political influence, the impact of China traders can easily be exaggerated.[26]

It is of course impossible to separate and weigh the relative importance of the various influences. Strategic considerations, however muddled, were in the forefront. Certainly the above evaluation implies no conspiracy by Roosevelt against the general welfare of the United States, but it does require us again to evaluate the military and political situation of the day, in light of what was known then and of what we know now.

On purely strategic grounds some observers might argue that the danger was not from Germany, Italy, or Japan alone, but rather from their combination in an aggressive alliance encircling the Western Hemisphere. The rhetoric of the time could suggest such a threat, but in fact the Tripartite Pact of Germany and Italy with Japan had become quite fragile. As explained in the preceding chapter, it was designed to deter United States entry into either of the then still-separate conflicts. The Japanese foreign minister in early 1941, Yosuke Matsuoka, had negotiated the Pact and was by far its strongest supporter in the cabinet. He tried to persuade his colleagues to follow the German attack on Russia with a similar

25. See Trefousse, *Germany,* p. 16, and William Appleman Williams, *The Tragedy of American Diplomacy* (New York: World, 1959).
26. See A. Whitney Griswold, *The Far Eastern Policy of the United States* (New York: Harcourt Brace, 1938).

act by Japan, but failed and was deposed. Thereafter the Pact faded in importance to the Tokyo government. In considering their subsequent negotiations with the United States the Japanese leaders were fully willing to sacrifice the Pact in return for the necessary economic concessions. Had Hitler managed to get himself into war with America in the Atlantic he could not successfully have invoked the Pact unless the Japanese clearly had seen war to be in their own interests.

Moreover, this drift away from Germany was, it has been well argued, adequately known to American and British officials—Ambassadors Grew and Craigie, Cordell Hull, Roosevelt and Churchill—thanks in part to American ability to crack the codes used in all Japanese secret cables. "After Matsuoka's fall . . . no Axis leader was able even to keep up the pretense of expecting Japanese intervention in behalf of Germany and Italy."[27] In the context of late 1941, therefore, the prospects of close cooperation among Germany, Italy and Japan were not very menacing. Given their very diverse long-run interests, and Hitler's racial notions, a "permanent" alliance surely does not seem very plausible. A special irony of the situation is that Roosevelt was particularly anxious to see Hitler beaten first, and that British and Dutch colonial possessions in Southeast Asia, which seemed essential to the European war, be unmolested. His belated insistence on Japanese evacuation from China then pushed the Axis back together and endangered his other goals.

Would Japanese success in China alone, without reference to their allies, have posed such a long-term threat as has sometimes been imagined? It is easy subconsciously to invoke old Western fears that still plague American China policy. Even limited to the home islands, after two decades of spectacular growth Japan today has the world's third largest GNP.

27. Schroeder, *Axis Alliance*, p. 155, also pp. 154–67 passim. Schroeder establishes Churchill and the Ambassadors' knowledge of the estrangement, and although he has less evidence for Hull and Roosevelt is nevertheless quite confident. Other recent books supporting this argument that a halt to Japanese expansion in China could have been obtained without the Pacific War include Ike, *Japan's Decision*, and John Toland, *The Rising Sun* (New York: Random House, 1970).

Yet it is only about one-sixth as large as that of the United States, and a third of Russia's. This third-ranking power is still manifestly weaker than the United States, as it was in 1941. From a thirty year perspective it is hard to argue that the great war made much ultimate difference either way in Japan's potential power in the world.

Firm Japanese control of all China would of course be a different matter, and would indeed have put at Tokyo's disposal an empire of awesome size. Still, really what are the prospects that Imperial Japan could effectively have ruled a population seven times larger than her own? Herbert Hoover at the time urged:

> We must remember some essentials of Asiatic life . . . that while Japan has the military ascendancy today and no doubt could take over parts or all of China, yet the Chinese people possess transcendent cultural resistance; that the mores of the race have carried through a dozen foreign dynasties over the 3,000 years . . . No matter what Japan does . . . they will not Japanify China and if they stay long enough they will be absorbed or expelled by the Chinese. For America to undertake this on behalf of China might expedite it, but would not make it more inevitable.[28]

The Japanese War in China was going so badly in 1941 that it seems rather far-fetched to imagine firm domination ever being established. Japan was already bogged down on the Asian mainland, as other powers have done since. The Chinese nationalists, and the Communists, probably could have continued to resist for years with continuing American and Russian military assistance short of war. Maybe not, but even so it would seem that there would have been substantial warning, still allowing the United States to institute a tough policy against the Japanese later on when the evidence was clear.

28. R. L. Wilbur and A. M. Hyde, *The Hoover Policies* (New York: Scribners, 1937), p. 600. Quoted in Isaacs, *Scratches*, p. 166.

4

From the North Atlantic
to the Tonkin Gulf

Nonbelligerent assistance

In retrospect, the fear that America would be left alone in
the world against two great victorious empires in Europe and
Asia seems terribly exaggerated. Clear-cut victory was not in
prospect for either, nor does the assumption that they could
long have maintained a close alliance seem especially plausible. The critical American mistake may well have been in
backing the Japanese into a corner, for without war in the
Pacific the American conflict with Germany very possibly
could have been held to limited naval engagements, but no
clash of ground troops. In short, we might at most have
fought a limited war.

These conclusions are highly speculative; the situation of
the time cannot be reproduced for another run, searching for
an alternate future. Perhaps I underestimate the risks that an
American determination to avoid war would have entailed.
On the other hand, the proposition that the war was unnecessary—in a real sense premature, fought before the need was
sufficiently clearly established, though the need might well
have become apparent later—is worth considering. Just possibly the isolationists were right in their essential perspective.

This last may be unpalatable, especially because the intellectual company of some of the most famous isolationists—
William Borah, Hiram Johnson, and Burton Wheeler—is not

very distinguished. Others like Father Coughlin were home-grown fascists, or, like Charles Lindbergh, are remembered as naive admirers of Germany. But once more, I do not imagine that the United States should have carried on blithely in 1941 as though nothing were happening elsewhere in the world. Complete isolation would have been much worse than intervention. All Americans would agree that American strategic interests required substantial assistance to the belligerents against Germany. Both Britain and Russia had to be preserved as independent and powerful states. With a little less certainty I would also grant the need to keep a significant portion of China viable.

It seems, however, that those goals could have been achieved by the belligerents themselves, with great American economic and noncombatant military aid. As insurance, American rearmament had to go on. A sustained defense effort not less than what was later accepted during the cold war would have been required. That would imply 10 percent of the American GNP devoted to military purposes, as compared with about that amount actually expended in 1941 and a mere one and one-half percent in 1939. That much, incidentally, would with Lend-Lease have been quite enough to revive the economy from the depression and assuredly does not imply idle resources.

With this prescription I find myself at odds with the extreme critics of Roosevelt's policy, men who spoke at that time and again, briefly, after the war. Most of the President's military and economic acts seem appropriate and, indeed, necessary. I have no quarrel with the decisions for rearmament or to institute Selective Service, with revision of the Neutrality Act to permit "cash-and-carry" by belligerents (effectively by the Allies only), with the destroyers-for-bases exchange, with Lend-Lease, or with the decision to convoy American vessels as far as Iceland. Even the famous "shoot-on-sight" order, even as interpreted to allow American destroyers to seek out the sight of U-boats, seems necessary if the convoys were to be protected on the first stage of the critical lifeline to Britain. I do have some serious reservations about the way in which those decisions were publicly justified, a matter for discussion below. But the content of those decisions seems fully defensible. And irritating as they surely were, Hitler would probably have continued to tolerate them in preference to more active American involvement.

Only two major exceptions to the content of American policy in 1941 appear worth registering. One is the vote by Congress in mid-November 1941, at the President's behest, removing nearly all the remaining restrictions of the Neutrality Act. It permitted American ships to carry supplies all the way across the Atlantic, instead of merely as far as Iceland. This almost certainly would have been too much for Hitler to bear. Had he allowed American ships to claim the benefits of neutrality and arrive unmolested in Britain, his entire effort to force British capitulation by naval warfare would have collapsed. The more American, rather than British, vessels carried cargoes the more ineffective the submarine campaign would have become. The situation would have required great self-restraint—a trait for which Hitler was not noted—and a willingness on all sides to envision a compromise peace as the outcome. Probably that willingness could not have emerged so quickly. More likely Hitler would have felt obliged to order his submarine commanders to attack all American shipping, instead of merely replying if attacked by American escort ships. The change would have precipitated heavy American merchant losses rather than just the occasional incident, usually involving warships, implied by the previous policy. That in turn might well have demanded more self-restraint by Roosevelt than was possible in the American political system, even if he had wanted very badly to avoid war. In short, the new American policy probably would have led in a few months to open, declared conflict. But as to whether that final step was necessary, as part of a plan to preserve an independent Britain for an ultimate negotiated settlement, I remain unconvinced.

The other and still more serious exception I take is with

President Roosevelt's policy toward Japan as described in the previous chapter. It was neither necessary nor desirable for him to have insisted on a Japanese withdrawal from China. An agreement for a standstill would have been enough, and he did not make an honest diplomatic attempt to achieve it. He refused to meet Prince Konoye in the Pacific to work out a compromise, and after Konoye's fall he rejected, on Hull's advice, a draft proposal that could have served as a basis for compromise with the Japanese. We have no guarantee that agreement could have been reached, but there was at least some chance and the effort was not made.

Worst case analysis

Several very serious objections to my view of a viable American policy can still be offered. The first is that I have minimized the dangers that would have been implied by a successful American effort to stay out of the war. My reply is essentially that the fundamental power balance in the world was more stable than many thought it to be. More generally, the argument could be extended to the cold war period, when I think we often took on the Chicken Little syndrome, exaggerating the threat to that stability in the face of every immediate crisis, coup, or distant war. ("The sky is falling! Run and tell the President!") Roosevelt's own words, though exaggerated, may have even more value than he thought: "We have nothing to fear but fear itself."

Cold war, and especially overt international violence, provides a condition of heightened fears, a fog of war in which everyone is especially likely to overrate the threat an enemy constitutes. At the beginning of World War II, for instance, British and American intelligence estimates of German war production were exaggerated by 50 to 100 percent.[1]

1. Klein, *Germany's Economic Preparations,* pp. 101–02.

In 1941 perhaps any possibility, however slim, of a true German *victory* was so undesirable as to justify intervention. Neither that nightmare, nor the retrospective chance of a Nazi government equipped with nuclear weapons, is one with which Americans could rest complacently. But we must always weigh possible outcomes by what we think is the probability that they will occur. Otherwise we fall victim to "worst case analysis," always trying desperately to avoid the worst regardless of how unlikely it is to happen even without our efforts. Death or mangling in a traffic accident is a possibility every time we step into an automobile. Most of us are nevertheless usually willing to take that risk rather than accept the far more likely losses to be incurred by giving up normal mobility for business and pleasure. Yet in analyzing international politics we sometimes forget this lesson.

During the past decade, members of the Administration in Washington decided that if a Viet Cong government ever took power in Saigon it might well set in motion a row of falling dominoes throughout Southeast Asia, as one non-Communist government after another tumbled. Before long the result might have been a set of Chinese or Russian-dominated governments, hostile to American interests, in the entire area. To avoid such an undesirable outcome they introduced a massive American military force. What was perhaps not asked, however, was whether another outcome which even they would consider nearly as undesirable—the quagmire—was even more likely to happen in the event of intervention than was the fall of dominoes in the absence of American military action. Thus by seeking to foreclose one very bad but improbable outcome in Asia the United States government made another one much more likely. Such action was probably encouraged by a simple-minded, and erroneous, use of the game theory principle of "minimax." That principle advises one to choose a strategy so as to minimize the chance of getting the outcome you regard as worst—but properly understood it does not mean bending all efforts to avoid very bad but very improbable events.

What is more, no comprehensive analysis of the broader costs and gains of fighting in Vietnam seems to have been made anywhere in the government. Narrow quantitative studies of body counts and controlled hamlets, made by systems analysts in the Pentagon, have been much blamed for the Vietnam fiasco. True, they often were naive or based on fabricated "information." Yet in a myopic perspective of systems analysis the Vietnam war can be considered something of a success. The minimal goal, to maintain an anti-Communist government in Saigon, has been met for a decade despite the incompetence and unpopularity of that government. A *narrow* analysis of military and political conditions necessary to achieve such an outcome would not deal with the broader political, economic, and moral costs of the war, to Vietnam and to the United States. It is the job of analysts elsewhere in the decision-making system—in the White House, the State Department—even Congress and the academic community—to measure those broader costs and to weigh their acceptability. But of course that broader evaluation was never properly undertaken either by policy-makers or by social scientists. Nor indeed was anything like such an analysis undertaken at the time of American entry into World War II. Strategic and political assumptions about the postwar world were left for improvisation or retrospective rancor.

Naval action in the North Atlantic, with American destroyers dropping depth-charges on German submarines and receiving torpedoes in turn, constituted America's first limited war. Another objection is that such a war could not, politically, have long continued. No doctrine for fighting limited war existed. Americans thought peace and war to be antithetical. Woodrow Wilson had felt impelled, despite his preferences, to declare war on Germany in 1917 over the issue of unrestricted submarine warfare. Very possibly it would have proved politically impossible to sustain long a policy of limited war in 1941 and 1942. The experience of the 1950s in which Americans did fight such a war against hundreds of thousands of Chinese troops, was still in the future—though it was to demonstrate how a conflict could be controlled if the will was there. The scenario I have put forth for the 1940s, one of rearmament, assistance, but careful avoidance of belligerency barring a true collapse of one of the major allies, would have required enormous political skill and possibly a quality of political support that did not exist in the country. Perhaps any idea of "fighting to the last ally" would have been too "cynical" to survive public debate. A few isolationists opposed both rearmament and aid to the allies, both of which were essential pillars in the policy I suggest. This last difficulty particularly demanded a candid discussion of foreign policy options, a discussion that Roosevelt never really led.

A broad coalition

Nevertheless, it is a mistake to lump all "isolationists" together as uniform advocates of a single policy. The opponents of American participation in the war included such a diverse lot as Oswald Garrison Villard, Socialist leader Norman Thomas, economist Stuart Chase, University of Chicago President Robert Hutchins, progressive Senators Borah, Johnson, LaFollette, and Wheeler, United Mine Workers leader John L. Lewis, former President Hoover, and conservative Senators like Robert A. Taft and Arthur Vandenberg. (The breadth of the antiintervensionist coalition in 1940 suggests the possibility of a similar broad-based coalition, including many from the right, emerging against intervention in the 1970s.) Certainly they all shared the view that Germany and Japan did not constitute a clear and present military danger to the United States. But many "isolationists" supported most or all of the proposed military buildup; the others offered no substantial opposition. Lindbergh wanted to "arm to the teeth." As one historian has told us:

Isolationists displayed no unanimity in their stand on specific defense measures. They made no concerted effort to block expansion of America's armed forces, however. Many isolationists, in fact, became ardent champions of the strongest possible defense and, occasionally, outdid the Administration in their efforts to improve America's military capabilities.[2]

With a single exception to be explained shortly, during the years 1939–1941 army and navy appropriations passed virtually unanimously, despite the numerical strength of those in Congress who opposed entry into the war. Most isolationists even were willing to give some aid to Britain. They opposed Lend-Lease, but proposed instead a two-billion dollar loan to help the British war effort, as a less sweeping commitment. A financial loan would not give the president power, as Lend-Lease did, to integrate the American economy with the British war effort, nor would it tempt him to act with American naval forces so as to insure the safe arrival of actual goods to be lent or leased.[3] Whether the substitute represented a deep-seated willingness to maintain Britain, or merely a political response from a desire to appear positive, is unimportant. The necessary political base for some substantial assistance to the British and later the Russians was there. And from many quarters Roosevelt heard the advice that while doing so, and fortifying the Western Hemisphere, he should allow Germany and Russia to exhaust each other.

Only two kinds of preparedness measures proposed by the Administration were fought by many isolationists; some naval construction, and Selective Service. The opposition to certain naval expenditures came early, in 1938, and faded thereafter. It stemmed from fears that a big navy would only be used to involve the United States in a distant war. This in turn was rooted in a long-term suspicion by many liberal isolationists

2. Jonas, *Isolationism*, pp. 129–30.
3. Warren I. Cohen, *The American Revisionists* (Chicago: University of Chicago Press, 1967), pp. 241–43.

of foreign trade and investments as a source of danger. Charles Beard saw the United States as potentially able to achieve economic near-sufficiency; he feared a big navy would be demanded to defend trade and therefore wanted trade reduced to a minimum.[4] Similarly, the Naval Construction Bill of 1939 initially included appropriations for developing the base on Guam. The isolationists feared such an act would antagonize the Japanese—but they did not oppose similar funds for projects on Wake and Midway Islands, closer to the United States. They wanted a navy capable of protecting the Western Hemisphere, but not able to embark on further adventures.[5] Opposition to renewal of Selective Service in 1941 centered less on the draft than on the possibility that conscripts might be sent overseas.

Thus the political climate was not nearly so hostile to rearmament and aid short of war as we may imagine. The same can be said of the public at large. As early as January 1939, a Gallup poll found 65 percent of the population anxious to spend more for defense. Throughout 1941 approximately the same proportion consistently, in repeated polls, were solidly in favor of aid to Britain. In fact, they declared it was "more important to help England than to keep out of war." Almost every survey found more than half the population approving Roosevelt's actions in helping Britain; another 20 percent felt he had not gone far enough.[6] Franklin Roosevelt therefore was pursuing a policy that was both politically

4. Jonas, *Isolationism*, p. 133. Also see Cohen, *American Revisionists*, pp. 129–34.

5. See *The Open Door at Home* (New York: Macmillan, 1935), esp. pp. 213–14. Several years ago in "The Calculus of Deterrence," *Journal of Conflict Resolution* 7, no. 2 (June 1963): 97–109, I pointed out evidence that if a small power was attacked, a big power defender was much more likely to honor its previous commitment to come to its rescue if there were close economic ties between the two. At that time I was concerned about strengthening Atlantic deterrence against Soviet attack, and thought promoting trade thus to have desirable political results.

6. Hadley Cantril, *The Human Dimension: Experiences in Policy Research* (New Brunswick, New Jersey: Rutgers University Press, 1967), pp. 47, 50.

viable and sufficient to keep the Allies in the war. Only toward the end of 1941, in dealing with both Germany and
Japan, did his decisions lead inevitably to war.

The cost of intervention

If American intervention in World War II was otherwise
avoidable and unnecessary, then what were its costs? I do not
think participation was a grave error in the sense that most
Americans are very much worse off, in directly traceable
consequence, than they otherwise would be. But the costs
were serious and must be set against the presumed gains.

American battle casualties were *relatively* light—fewer
than 300,000 men killed, a figure less than 10 percent of
German losses, or less than 5 percent of Russian military
casualties alone. Yet that many deaths can hardly be forgotten. Furthermore, in World War II the United States used
up important natural resources, especially oil and metals, that
can never be replaced. For example, America is now dependent on imports of iron ore following exhaustion of the
great Mesabi iron range in Minnesota. The dream of continental self-sufficiency was much less far-fetched to the isolationists of 1940 than it can ever be again, in part because
of the exertions World War II imposed. A greater loss is probably the damage to the world's physical environment which
the conduct of World War II accelerated and which we have
continued with the preparations for further wars.

Moreover, World War II left some undesirable legacies in
American thought patterns. One may be the illusion that
Asians can always be beaten in war, even when the main
American effort is concentrated on the European theatre. Another may be a habit of intervention, of putting American
military effort prematurely into the scales to prevent the
buildup of hostile power even in the remote future. Nothing
fails like success. And the strategy of gradual escalation of

pressures against a weaker opponent, applied so disastrously to Japan, returned in Vietnam.

Yet another is the corrupting effect actual conduct of the conflict had on our view of what constituted morally permissible acts in warfare. For the first year of the war urban areas of the major combatants were largely spared. (There were some exceptions for the smaller states, notably the case of Rotterdam in May 1940.) President Roosevelt characterized the earliest, and mildest, German air attacks as "inhuman barbarism that has profoundly shocked the conscience of humanity."[7] But as the war dragged on German planes bombed British cities in the Blitz and the British habitually attacked German urban centers at night when precision bombing was impossible, deliberately directing many of their strikes against residential areas for their effect on popular morale. Another myth that needs revision is that the Germans initiated such attacks; on the contrary, Churchill can also be give some credit for the breakdown of previous restraints on bombing civilians.[8] American bombing raids on Germany as a rule—though there were notable exceptions—attempted to concentrate on industrial targets and were largely conducted during daylight hours.

But if Americans can claim a few credits for restraint in the air war over Europe, the firebomb raids on Japanese cities (in which a ring of fire was carefully built to trap people inside) remove much virtue from that account. The horrors of Hiroshima and Nagasaki were a direct outgrowth of the firebombing precedent. After the war all restraints were forgotten. On the basis of their own actions against Japan, American military planners simply assumed that in future wars nuclear weapons would be used against cities to destroy the enemy's economy, society, and popular morale. This strategy was basically unquestioned until the late 1950s, in

7. Quoted in Robert E. Osgood and Robert W. Tucker, *Force, Order, and Justice* (Baltimore: Johns Hopkins Press, 1967), p. 217.
8. George Quester, *Deterrence Before Hiroshima* (New York: Wiley, 1966), pp. 105–22.

other countries as well as in the United States. It remains essentially in force, and thus the current ever-present nuclear threat to American cities is an inheritance from our, and other nations', acts in World War II.

Another direct legacy has been the American conduct of war from the air in South Vietnam, napalming villages and suburban areas and the leveling of large tracts of the city of Hué. Nor were the corruptions of war limited to the behavior of airmen. Atrocities committed by Americans against Japanese, as well as vice-versa, gave frightening premonitions of My Lai.[9] American soldiers commonly refused to take prisoners in the Pacific.

Material costs too must be considered. Even at the end of the New Deal some contemporary observers thought that military preparations endangered continued attention to American domestic needs. The "continentialists," in the words of two of them, objected to:

lecturing other nations, constantly stirring up in effect, warlike emotions, and using the power of the United States to force any scheme of politics or economy on other peoples. They especially opposed, as distracting and dangerous to domestic life, the propagation of the idea that any mere foreign policy could in any material respect reduce the amount of degrading poverty in the United States, set the American economy in full motion, or substantially add to the well-being of the American people. Foreign policy, they held, could easily be made the instrument to stifle domestic wrongs under a blanket of militarist chauvinism, perhaps disguised by the high-sounding title of world peace.[10]

There is an unfortunate coincidence between participation in war and the death of attempts at domestic reform in the

9. For example, see Charles Lindbergh's observations on duty in the South Pacific, in *The Wartime Journals of Charles A. Lindbergh* (New York: Harcourt Brace Jovanovich, 1970).

10. Charles A. Beard and Mary R. Beard, *America in Mid-passage* (New York: Macmillan, 1939), p. 455.

twentieth century. World War I marked the end of Wilson's New Freedom. Lyndon Johnson's War on Poverty was one of the first casualties of his war on the Viet Cong. And World War II, on top of the 1938 election, ended the New Deal.

True enough, the United States has undertaken heavy and long-term military efforts without the emergence of a Garrison State. Yet the American economy, and the political system, have paid a real price for heavy military expenditure in an atmosphere of grave external threat. On the material side, these costs include a relative neglect of physical and social investment. Military expenditure has to come at the expense of some other kind of spending, public or private. Over the past 30 years, some of the price has indeed been paid by immediate personal consumption. But proportionately the impact on investment—capital formation—has been very much greater. Public spending for education and health have suffered heavily too, and these statements apply to the exertions of World War II as well as to the cold war years. Americans are somewhat poorer, more ignorant, and less healthy than they would be if the military spending had not been necessary, or deemed necessary.

The feeling of need for constant vigilance against threats, domestic as well as foreign, represents a political cost. At least some kinds of military spending are closely associated with "conservative," hawkish, strongly anticommunist attitudes among our political leaders. Legislators whose states benefit from disproportionate shares of spending for military installations are quite likely to be foreign policy hard-liners. The effect of heavy military spending is to shift the nation's political center of gravity to the right.

Similarly, the devastation of previous strong restraints on military spending can be traced to the World War II period. Before 1939 the armed forces included only about a quarter of a million men. The country had a tradition of close scrutiny of military budgets and suspicion of peacetime army that was very different from the latitude given the armed forces during the cold war. But at no point since the end of the war have fewer than 1,400,000 Americans been under arms. Of course, the cold war and Soviet-American arms race were substantially responsible for this development, but a standard American pattern of wartime military expansion and only partial postwar contraction was also at work. The Spanish-American War, World War I, and the Korean War each produced a virtual and permanent doubling of the armed forces over the size characteristic of the preceding years. And it is not enough simply to invoke the image of objective global responsibilities after each war. While that explanation surely has some truth, Parkinson's Law also comes to mind. So too does an image of a political system where each war weakened the restraints on the activities of military men and their civilian allies. World War II, which lasted 44 months for the United States and at its peak absorbed more than 40 percent of the national product, unavoidably built a "military-industrial complex" that could not easily be dismantled at war's end.[11] Similarly, the prosecution of the war required a system of higher taxes and governmental control of the economy and society that has never been entirely dismantled.

In fairness, however, my alternative scenario for 1941 would have required heavy defense spending and some of these same costs as were incurred by fighting World War II. Whether the system has been more "healthy" with a great war and then cold war from 1946 onward is subject only to speculation. I am nevertheless inclined to believe that some of the excesses of the cold war period have their roots in the World War II experience. One of the greatest anxieties of liberal isolationists about intervention was that it would permanently restrict political freedoms at home, that American democracy could not survive sustained militarization. On April 13, 1940, the *New York Times* quoted Beard as accusing J. Edgar Hoover of setting up a "political bureau" in the Department of Justice,

11. Evidence on the preceding paragraphs is presented in Bruce Russett, *What Price Vigilance? The Burdens of National Defense* (New Haven: Yale University Press, 1970).

for the purpose of indexing and spying upon persons charged with holding objectionable but not illegal views in matters of politics and economics, or engaging in activities of which he does not approve.[12]

Power and candor

The years 1940 and 1941 marked the first great exercise of a president's powers as Commander-in-Chief during peacetime. They represent a period when secret military planning with the British became extremely close, and when American naval forces were committed to actions that were sure to involve them in hostilities. Restraints on the president's execution of foreign policy loosened and have never been restored. A good deal of controversy over Roosevelt's intentions raged during the 1940s, and still has not entirely abated. Some extreme revisionists who published immediately after the war accused him of *seeking* war with Germany and Japan, and of deliberately inviting the Japanese attack on Pearl Harbor.

Most historians reject these extreme interpretations. Such charges about intentions probably can never be substantiated or conclusively disproved, and they have distracted us from more important questions like the one posed in this essay— regardless of intentions, was the conflict in fact necessary? One standard interpretation seems to be that Roosevelt decided at some point, perhaps several years before Pearl Harbor, that the United States would have to go to war. But isolationist sentiment was so powerful that he felt unable to present the issue squarely to the people, and so proceeded cautiously, step-by-step, to help the Allies as much as Congress and the electorate would permit. According to this

12. Cited in Cohen, *American Revisionists*, p. 226.

interpretation he is to be faulted for never having frankly discussed his private conviction that the United States should go to war to prevent Axis domination, and the implications of his policy.

Some aspects of his leadership seem chillingly familiar to those of us who have since listened to Lyndon Johnson, Robert McNamara, and Dean Rusk discuss their intentions in Vietnam. The most famous incident occurred in FDR's October 30 campaign address to an Irish-American audience in Boston, when he declared, "I have said this before, but I shall say it again, and again, and again. Your boys are not going to be sent into any foreign wars." At the time he did worry a bit whether he could keep this promise, but decided that the phrase "foreign wars" was too ambiguous to bind him. To his speech-writer he remarked, "If we're attacked it's no longer a foreign war."[13]

Even so, we cannot judge Roosevelt guilty of duplicity on this evidence. Most observers feel that he still did not believe his assistance to Britain would lead to all-out war, but rather continued to hope that British resistance, sustained by America, would be enough to hold Hitler back. One historian who has carefully considered the question remarks about Lend-Lease, despite its almost unprecedentedly nonneutral nature: ". . . the president felt with great sincerity that this policy would not lead to American involvement but to a British victory that alone would keep the nation out of war." And later, "His own personal hatred of war was deep and genuine, and it was this conviction that set him apart from men like Stimson and Morgenthau, who decided that American par-

___

13. Samuel I. Rosenman, *Working with Roosevelt* (New York: Harper and Row, 1952), p. 242. Many writers have pointed to his famous speech in 1937 calling for a "quarantine" of the aggressors as evidence of an early and strong determination to resist even at great cost. Recent evidence makes it appear unlikely that any such determination was present. See Dorothy Borg, "Notes on Roosevelt's 'Quarantine' Speech," in Robert A. Divine, ed., *Causes and Consequences of World War II* (Chicago: Quadrangle, 1969), p. 47–70.

ticipation was necessary in the spring of 1941 . . . It is quite possible that Roosevelt never fully committed himself to American involvement prior to Pearl Harbor."[14]

But if Roosevelt is acquitted of these charges, it is not possible to let him off so easily for his acts on two other occasions. He certainly was not above manipulating the facts about naval incidents in the North Atlantic, in a way that provided a perfect precedent for his successor a generation later. In September 1941 a German submarine fired two torpedoes, both missing, at the American destroyer *Greer*. President Roosevelt responded, in a radio broadcast, with the following description to the event as an act of "piracy": The *Greer*

> was carrying American mail to Iceland. . . . I tell you the blunt fact that the German submarine fired first upon this American destroyer without warning, and with deliberate design to sink her . . .
>
> We have sought no shooting war with Hitler. We do not seek it now. But neither do we want peace so much that we are willing to pay for it by permitting him to attack our naval and merchant ships while they are on legitimate business.[15]

It later emerged that the "legitimate business" was that the *Greer* "had been following the U-Boat for more than three hours and had been broadcasting its position to nearby British naval units."[16]

The second incident occurred the following month when the destroyer *Kearny* was torpedoed. Although the ship was not sunk, eleven American sailors were killed. In his subsequent radio address Roosevelt declared:

---

14. Robert A. Divine, *Roosevelt and World War II* (Baltimore: Penguin, 1970), pp. 40, 47–48.
15. *New York Times*, September 12, 1941, pp. 1, 4.
16. Divine, *Roosevelt*, p. 44.

We have wished to avoid shooting. But the shooting
has started. And history has recorded who fired the first
shot . . .

America has been attacked. The U.S.S. *Kearny* is not
just a navy ship. She belongs to every man, woman, and
child in this Nation. . . . Hitler's torpedo was directed
at every American, whether he lives on our seacoast or
in the innermost part of the Nation far from the sea and
far from the guns and tanks of the marching hordes of
would-be-conquerors of the world.

The purpose of Hitler's attack was to frighten the
American people off the high seas—to force us to make
a trembling retreat.[17]

What really happened in this incident, where "history has
recorded the first shot," was described two days later in a
formal report by Secretary of the Navy Knox:

On the night of October 16–17 the U.S.S. *Kearny*
while escorting a convoy of merchant ships received dis-
tress signals from another convoy which was under
attack from several submarines. The U.S.S. *Kearny* proceeded to the aid of the attacked convoy. On arriving at
the scene of the attack the U.S.S. *Kearny* dropped depth
bombs when she sighted a merchant ship under attack
by a submarine.[18]

Compare these statements of Roosevelt with those of President Johnson in August 1964, after two naval incidents in the
Tonkin Gulf:

This new act of aggression aimed directly at our forces
again brings home to all of us in the United States the
importance of the struggle for peace and security in
Southeast Asia.

17. *New York Times*, October 28, 1941, p. 4.
18. Ibid., October 30, p. 1.

Aggression by terror against peaceful villages of South Vietnam has now been joined by open aggression on the high seas against the United States of America . . . We Americans know—although others appear to forget—the risk of spreading conflict. We still seek no wider war.[19]

Lyndon Johnson was an avowed admirer of Franklin Roosevelt, and a young New Dealer before the war. Did he, or his speechwriter, consciously draw on the earlier experience? Certainly he failed to mention the clandestine American-sponsored air-attacks and South Vietnamese naval actions against the North Vietnam coast that had been conducted prior to the Tonkin Gulf Resolution. If Hanoi interpreted the American destroyers' presence in the Gulf as part of those actions, then its response was something less than "open aggression." Yet Johnson's reply was a severe air strike, then the predrafted Tonkin Gulf Resolution and ultimately full-scale American intervention. In the subsequent election campaign he lashed his opponent's advocacy of a bombing campaign even though his Administration had reached a consensus that heavy air attacks on the North would in fact be necessary.[20]

In this context it is worth quoting once again from Charles Beard who, though extreme and sometimes blind in his hatred of Roosevelt, uttered some ringing prophecies. If Roosevelt's acts stand as precedent, he warned,

The President of the United States in a campaign for reelection may publicly promise the people to keep the country out of war and, after victory at the polls, may set out secretly on a course designed or practically certain to bring war upon the country.

He may, to secure legislation in furtherance of his secret designs, misrepresent to Congress and the people

19. *New York Times*, August 5, 1964, p. 1.
20. See *The Pentagon Papers* as edited by the *New York Times* (New York: Bantam, 1971), Chapters 5 and 6.

both its purport and the policy he intends to pursue under its terms if and when such legislation is enacted . . .

He may publicly represent to Congress and the people that acts of war have been committed against the United States, when in reality the said acts were secretly invited and even initiated by the armed forces of the United States under his secret direction.[21]

Without accepting the most insidious charges of those who attacked Franklin Roosevelt, it is nevertheless clear that his actions as Commander-in-Chief, for a cause that was generally popular, made similar acts by his successors much easier. Recall again some of his initiatives, not submitted to Congress: the destroyers-for-bases exchange by an executive agreement more important than almost all of the nearly one thousand treaties that have been submitted to the Senate; the order to American forces to occupy Iceland; the order that American warships should convoy British as well as American vessels in the North Atlantic, and later to "shoot on sight" —and to seek out—German submarines. In these interpretations of his power Roosevelt was hardly timid. Even one, like this author, who considers these steps, at least, to have been in the immediate American interest, has some qualms. We can allow one of Roosevelt's firm sympathizers to sum up the argument, though we may reach a different verdict:

Franklin Roosevelt repeatedly deceived the American people during the period before Pearl Harbor . . . He was like the physician who must tell the patient lies for the patient's own good. . . . A president who cannot entrust the people with the truth betrays a certain lack of faith in the basic tenets of democracy. But because the masses are notoriously shortsighted and generally cannot see danger until it is at their throats, our statesmen are forced to deceive them into an awareness of

21. Charles A. Beard, *President Roosevelt and the Coming of War, 1941* (New Haven: Yale University Press, 1948), pp. 582–84.

their own long-run interests. This is clearly what Roosevelt had to do, and who shall say that posterity will not thank him for it?[22]

Roosevelt, like Johnson after him, not only was uncandid, but made his decisions within a small circle of intimate advisers.

No more Munichs

The theme of the above quotation, "the masses are notoriously shortsighted and generally cannot see danger until it is at their throats," is typical of thousands of writers and political figures. Preventive medicine was the prescription; dangers must be faced at their inception, while the threat is still small enough to be controlled. The lesson of Munich had to be learned. The Allies had waited until very nearly too late to stand up to Hitler; that mistake must not be repeated. Stalin had the same kind of insatiable ambitions as Hitler, thus he must be stopped at the beginning. It is astonishing how often, immediately after the war or even while it still continued, Americans applied, or misapplied, the "lessons" of dealing with Hitler.

Some samples of the equation of Stalin with Hitler include James Forrestal, reporting Averell Harriman's comments that

the outward thrust of communism was not dead and that we might well have to face an ideological warfare just as vigorous and dangerous as fascism or Nazism.[23]

22. Thomas A. Bailey, *The Man in the Street* (New York: Macmillan, 1948), p. 13. Among many others who share essentially this conclusion, a little less approvingly, are Richard Hofstadter, *The Progressive Historians: Turner, Beard and Parrington* (New York: Knopf, 1968), pp. 336–37, and Robert E. Osgood, *Ideals and Self-Interest in America's Foreign Relations* (Chicago: University of Chicago Press, 1953), p. 412.
23. Walter Millis, ed., *The Forrestal Diaries* (New York: Viking, 1951), p. 47. Diary entry of April 20, 1945.

Forrestal himself, sending Henry Luce a study by Edward Willett of the "real moral and philosophical foundations of the Russian State":

> I realize it is easy to ridicule the need for such a study as I have asked Willett to make, but in the middle of that laughter we always should remember that we also laughed at Hitler.[24]

Harry Truman remarked that

> the new menace facing us seemed every bit as grave as Nazi Germany and her allies had been.[25]

and James Byrnes, Truman's secretary of state:

> they (Soviet leaders) must learn what Hitler learned— that the world is not going to permit one nation to veto peace on earth.[26]

Both Truman and Johnson, in their later military moves into Korea and Vietnam, explicitly invoked pre-World War II analogies. Truman's thoughts, on hearing about the North Korean attack, bear repeating:

> In my generation this was not the first occasion when the strong had attacked the weak. I recalled some earlier instances: Manchuria, Ethiopia, Austria. I remembered how each time that the democracies failed to act it had encouraged the aggressors to keep going ahead. Communism was acting in Korea just as Hitler, Mussolini, and the Japanese had acted ten, fifteen, twenty years earlier . . . If this was allowed to go unchallenged it

24. Ibid., p. 128.
25. Harry S. Truman, *Years of Trial and Hope* (Garden City, New York: Doubleday, 1956), p. 101.
26. James Byrnes, *Speaking Frankly* (New York: Harper and Row, 1947), p. 203.

would mean a third world war, just as similar incidents had brought on the second world war.[27]

Woodrow Wilson had reluctantly brought the United States into war in 1917, but because of pervasive isolationist sentiment the peace was lost. Americans refused to participate in a world collective security system, and allowed Germany to break the peace once more. Truman also recalled,

> I could never quite forget the strong hold which isolationism had gained over our country after World War I. . . . I had a very good picture of what a revival of American isolationism would mean for the world. . . . Inaction, withdrawal, "Fortress America" notions could only result in handing to the Russians vast areas of the globe now denied them.[28]

But after the second war the forces within America who opposed an interventionist policy were gravely depleted. Interventionists, having carried their policy to its seemingly glorious conclusion, could hardly question its applicability in a new situation. The arch-conservative isolationists of 1940 could now change sides. Whereas they had been unable to find much enthusiasm for war with Hitler, Communist Russia was quite another matter. And the liberal isolationists were disarmed. In the early years of the cold war all American liberals were required to demonstrate their loyalty and freedom from any taint of pro-Communism. Many of the most ardent reformers of the 1930s became the ardent cold warriors of the 1940s, what one wag called, in lower case letters, "national socialists." After embracing a hard-line cold war policy they had little incentive to question the wisdom of earlier global activism. In any case they strongly identified with Franklin Roosevelt, and so hastened to defend him from the exaggerated charges of his critics. Only a few eccentrics

27. Truman, *Trial and Hope*, pp. 332–33.
28. Ibid., pp. 101–02.

remained to challenge an activist "containment" foreign policy in either its past or its then-current form.

Revisionist historians of the First World War played no small part in the general revulsion from Europe's quarrels that swept the United States during the twenties. It was necessary to insure that a new isolationism was not fed as the old one had been. The possibility was slight anyway, but just to be certain a number of scholars, whose views on the war were known not to be seriously at odds with the Administration's, were provided with special access to individuals and to files. Most of these scholars had worked for the government during the war and could draw on their experiences and contacts. Others—and even some of these same scholars, years later after their access had expired—encountered the usual difficulties in trying to see classified documents.[29] Hence for a full generation a single approving view has held sway among most academics as well as in the public at large.

It would of course be unfair and inaccurate to trace all the developments cited in this chapter, and especially the adoption of interventionist policies, only back to 1940, just as it is wrong to think they emerged full-blown at the beginning of the cold war. One can find roots in our earlier Caribbean policy, in Woodrow Wilson's acts, in the war of 1898, and even earlier. But World War II, rather like monosodium glutamate, made pungent a host of unsavory flavors that had until then been relatively subdued. We cannot really extirpate contemporary "global policeman" conceptions from American thinking unless we understand how, in World War II, they developed and became deeply ingrained.

29. See Herbert Feis, "The Shackled Historian," *Foreign Affairs* 45, no. 2 (January 1967): 332–43.

5

Force and Choice in the Environment
of International Politics

A presumption against force

In the now-standard evaluations of American politics before
Pearl Harbor, it is agreed that the interventionists were the
realists who accepted war for *realpolitik*, to preserve the balance of power. As such they are contrasted both with the
Wilsonian idealists who went on crusade a generation before,
and with the isolationists whose true understanding of international politics is thought to have been hopelessly deficient.
Doubtless Roosevelt and his supporters tried to think objectively of the national interest in a more detached way than
had Woodrow Wilson, but it is not clear that they were correct in their strategic evaluations. Their thinking held elements of a sentimental attitude toward China, an anxiety to
protect American foreign trade and investment, extreme concern for the purity of American interest in Latin America
which fed fears of German influence there, oversimplified
Mahanist strategic notions and excessive worry about disposi-
tion of the British fleet, and an attachment to England that
allowed them to see the United States in Britain's traditional
role of balancer. Even a detailed intellectual history would be
unlikely to tell us how to weigh the importance of these elements, and it would be unwise to emphasize any of them. It
certainly is not possible to sort out the various motivations
here. Nevertheless—and especially in light of how dubious

the strategic justification appears—further inquiry is an important and necessary task.

What is sure is that the United States ultimately went to war, as a consequence of some theories that now seem inadequate. My discussion of the ill-effects of World War II is directed to the overall experience of having fought that war, not simply to the consequences of allegedly "losing" the peace to Russia as some have charged. The reader may not accept all the elements of this revisionist view. But if he agrees with much of it he may concur that, to a greater degree than has been true in American policy during recent decades, there must be an initial presumption against the use of force in international politics.

In the cold war period, the threat of violence often seemed the only available means for influencing America's antagonists because other potential means had been deliberately abandoned. This was most noticeable in American relations with Communist China, North Korea, and North Vietnam. When in the winter of 1968 the North Korean government seized the intelligence ship *Pueblo* and its crew, there was in fact nothing the United States could do to obtain their release. The threat or use of military force was impossible because of the circumstances: any resort to force would doom the crew at the hands of its captors. But since the United States had previously cut off all normal intercourse with the North Korean regime—diplomatic relations, trade, travel, cultural exchange all were suspended or had never existed—Washington had no bargaining levers. The circumstances were hardly appropriate for offering new carrots, and since the normal commerce of nations was nonexistent there were no carrots available to be withdrawn, or of which withdrawal could be threatened. Left with only the big stick, the stick's wielder was in fact impotent. And the North Koreans, knowing in advance how limited the range of options open to the United States would be, could plan their operation with confidence in its safety. How much more reluctant might they have been if they had had some stake in good relations with the United States, a stake to be lost by initiating hostile action?

Less dramatically but more importantly this same kind of limitation, an abandonment of most of the means of persuasion other than violence or its threat, has hampered the American government in its efforts to influence the rulers of Peking. Generally, political leaders, especially when dealing with states seen as predominantly hostile, tend to emphasize punishments and prohibitions. Opponents must be deterred, they must be presented with a high probability of pain if they commit acts of which we seriously disapprove. In holding such a view leaders are like the lawmaker who hopes to deter socially undesirable behavior solely through the threat of arrest and imprisonment.

That focus, however, ignores the simple fact that most people obey laws less from an overt fear of punishment than from habit, convenience, and a sense that to do so is accepted and in some way correct. When authority is no longer perceived as just, *only* coercion will enforce its wishes—but times are indeed hard when that happens. Law-abiding behavior is normally *rewarding* behavior; an effective lawmaker structures the situation so that people will do as he wishes as much because in some material or psychic way it rewards them as because undesired behavior will result in punishment.

Of course, the offer of rewards will not always be effective either. Sometimes it may be interpreted, perhaps correctly, as a sign of weakness and an encouragement to blackmail. Sometimes too, a previous emphasis on threat and violence may have so charged the atmosphere that the offer of reward is met only with contempt or suspicion. Such a condition undoubtedly existed at the time of President Johnson's apparent offer, in 1965, of massive development aid to the entire Mekong Valley area in Southeast Asia. The offer was particularly meant to include North Vietnam, but was quickly brushed aside by the Communists. By that time the offer was dismissed as just an imperialist bribe or an empty public relations gesture. It is much harder to force an opponent to *change* a policy already embarked upon than to *deter* such action before it has begun. A decade earlier, and before the war, an offer of American assistance might not have been received quite so negatively as it was later. The Hanoi government was in any case by 1965 deeply committed to assisting the Viet Cong, and a major reversal of policy would have caused great difficulties in its internal politics.

Imagine a scenario rather like this: After the French evacuated Indochina and signed the Geneva agreements calling at least temporarily for separate governments in North and South Vietnam, the United States could have recognized the North Vietnamese government in Hanoi. It really is not such a preposterous idea, considering that after all, the United States had not been fighting in Indochina and so there was no question therefore of recognizing a regime against which Americans had fought. At the same time, Washington might have encouraged trade with the new regime. Thus North Vietnam would not have been put on the strategic embargo list that forbade or sharply limited American trade with China, North Korea, the Soviet Union, and Eastern Europe. So long as the North Vietnamese did not break the embargo by shipping Western goods on to other Communist states, the United States might not only have permitted but actually have encouraged trade with Hanoi. Furthermore, some economic aid for reconstructing the economy might have been extended. In public statements the American government might have managed to say some complimentary things about "nationalist" Ho Chi Minh, deemphasing the fact that he also happened to be a Communist. The United States might have stressed, as it did, the fact of important differences between North and South Vietnam and the need for the government of the South to be independent of the North, but the tone could have been quite different. Instead of emphasizing anti-Communism and the ideological differences, it might instead have stressed the cultural, religious, and ethnic differences between the two halves, and how they had never really formed a unified nation.

The purpose of this strategy would have been to convey to the governments of both parts of Vietnam a desire to see South Vietnam remain independent, without directing strong condemnatory statements against the North. Instead of cutting virtually all the normal ties among nations, a rather substantial carrot would have been dangled before Hanoi to encourage peaceful relations with the South. The threat to withdraw the carrot in case of a Northern inspired or assisted effort to overthrow the Saigon government could have been made clearly enough implicitly, as could the ultimate intention to oppose any such effort militarily. But the primary effort would have been to soft-pedal threats and to build, over time, substantial positive incentives for the behavior desired by the American government. Note that such a policy is *not* one of appeasement. It does not consist in giving things away in the vague hope that the opponent will be satisfied; rather it expects concrete acts and concessions in return for those extended. Furthermore, the threat of force remains in the background should he prove unwilling to seek agreement.

Now as always with hindsight no one can say whether this policy would have worked, or even whether it was better than some other, such as accepting unification of the country from the beginning. But certainly the punishment-oriented policy that was tried brought no great success, and it is intriguing to speculate about the possibilities of a reward-oriented effort. Learning theory in psychology stresses rewards as well as punishments, and indeed under many conditions rewards for desired behavior are more effective than is punishment for undesired acts. Punishment, or threatened punishment, may make a decision-maker so fearful that it becomes hard for him to perceive alternatives or to weigh calmly the consequences of his action. As a result he may act rashly or "irrationally," perhaps doing just what the would-be deterrer wants him not to do.

An alternative far eastern policy in the thirties?

On the whole, American policy toward Japan in the 1930s consisted largely of punishments and threats. Secretary of State Henry L. Stimson greeted Japan's occupation of Manchuria with a determination to reverse it, even at substantial cost to the United States. He issued a declaration that the United States would recognize no territorial changes resulting from the war. Privately, he urged both President Hoover and the British government to impose economic sanctions to force the Japanese to withdraw, coupled with a willingness to accept war as a consequence if sanctions failed. Hoover and the British refused to support Stimson on a matter which did not, they considered, affect vital interests. So he was limited to a doctrine of nonrecognition as "moral suasion," which was of course effective in angering the Japanese without causing them in any way to reverse their actions. But a policy very much like that advocated by Stimson in 1932 was in fact adopted in 1940 and 1941—economic sanctions to halt (and then, more ambigously and dangerously, to reverse) Japanese occupation of China, even at the risk of a general Pacific war. Stimson applied the lessons of Manchuria as others did those of Munich.

By thinking largely in terms of threats the United States government was left on both occasions with policies that could not achieve their aims. But some officials did consider quite different strategies. In November 1941, for instance, a proposed economic policy was drawn up in the Treasury Department designed to discourage Japanese military expansion insofar as that expansion was economically motivated. It proposed to give the Japanese an opportunity to expand their markets in prosperity, without military occupation that would destroy the independence of Asian peoples or utterly exclude the western powers.

Accordingly the proposal included the following bargain: Japan should withdraw her military forces from all of China and probably Manchuria, and also from Indochina and Siam. It would recognize Chiang Kai-shek's government and surrender its extraterritorial rights in China. Economically, it would offer the Chinese a loan of a billion yen at two per cent interest, sell the United States as much as three-fourths of its current output of war materials, and accord the United States and China most-favored-nation treatment in trade.

Japan would cut its ties with the Axis and negotiate a mutual nonaggression pact with America, China, and Britain. These represented all the major goals of American far eastern policy at the time, in some cases to a degree not anticipated by the most optimistic Americans.

In turn, according to this proposal, the United States was to make important concessions to the Japanese. Like Japan, America would give up its extraterritorial rights in China and persuade the British to follow suit, and it would repeal the immigration laws discriminating against Asians. It would reciprocate the Japanese extension of most-favored-nation treatment, extend Tokyo a two billion dollar credit at two per cent interest, and try to assure Japan access to raw materials. Militarily it would withdraw the bulk of its naval forces from the Pacific.[1]

Secretary of the Treasury Henry Morgenthau was intrigued by the proposal, and sent it on to Secretary Hull at the State Department, who read it with some sympathy. Hull incorporated many of its components in his own draft for the President. Roosevelt also considered it for a while, but the Chinese government heard of it and reacted fearfully to what it called "appeasement." Roosevelt then put the plan aside as unrealistic. Probably it was, by then, almost as absurd as Johnson's much later development plan for the Mekong. Japanese-American relations had deteriorated so far into hostility and suspicion that no such settlement—in which trust would have to be a major component—was likely.

But it might not have seemed absurd earlier, especially back in 1932. At that point a comprehensive Japanese-American agreement that recognized legitimate economic and strategic interests of each might have been received much more favorably in both governments. Relations between them were not then so bad as to make the exercise pointless. In fact, on reading it one is struck with the similarity of many major points to what actually occurred after World War II—which

1. This description is taken from Blum, pp. 384–87. I am grateful to Blum for pointing out its possible applicability to the early 1930s.

America fought, in the Pacific, to diminish Japanese power. Japan certainly did give up its special privileges in China, the Axis was smashed, and the United States has, with other nations, obtained substantial (though by no means unrestricted) access to Japanese markets. On the other hand, the United States has also lost its economic position in China, it extended billions of dollars of economic aid for the reconstruction of Japan, and the national origin quotas of American immigration laws have been repealed. Japan is busy establishing a favorable trading relationship, if not with China, then throughout Southeast Asia.

It would be unfair to push this reasoning too far as criticism of actual American policy in the 1930s. The comprehensive settlement would have met with severe political opposition on emotional grounds and from entrenched economic and military interests in both countries. Probably in 1932 the need was not so obvious as to attract enough concentrated attention from busy men. And statesmen normally do not think this way, especially in terms of broad far-reaching agreements. But it was an alternative to force and the threat of force. Just because the United States government did not and perhaps even could not have pursued it must not keep us from considering the virtues of it and other alternatives under more favorable circumstances. It was an alternative between unilateral intervention and isolation, an overlooked item on a menu of conceivable choice. It illustrates a kind of international involvement intended to promote major national goals even with powers whose relationship to America initially contains important elements of hostility. It represents a kind of thinking that might now be revived as Americans and Chinese reconsider their policy toward each other. In a period when many fear a new isolationism, it may represent a sane option between "manic intervention and depressive withdrawal."[2]

2. The phrase is from James Patrick Sewell, "Functional Agencies," in Richard A. Falk and Cyril Black, *The Structure of the International Environment* (Princeton: Princeton University Press, 1971).

The menu of choice in foreign policy

What determines the range of choices potentially available to national decision-makers? What are the limits within which personality differences, bureaucratic roles, different theoretical perspectives, or alternative styles of bargaining and negotiation can affect choice? The distinction between the process of selection among alternatives and the set of choices offered is crucial to an understanding of current United States foreign policy dilemmas. If you walk into a restaurant, what you order of course depends on how hungry you are, your tastes, and how much money you have. It also depends on what the menu offers. Dinner at a pizza palace offering dozens of varieties of pizza is not likely to be very satisfactory if you don't happen to like pizza.

Not many Americans are very happy about the menu that has recently faced the United States in Indochina. Neither escalation nor withdrawal, in any of their possible permutations, nor continuing to slog on somewhere in between, looked very attractive. There was no "good" solution to the predicament, only a selection of more or less bad options. Now of course there were differences among Americans on just what the possible range of choice offered really was. Yet strong opposition to the war did not spread far beyond intellectual circles before 1968. Even then the range of realistic choice, as perceived by the general public, was not wide. While Gallup poll respondents had become as likely to refer to themselves as doves as hawks, few favored a unilateral withdrawal.[3] Though many would have preferred a somewhat different policy by their government, most had in mind matters of style and emphasis rather than a drastic shift. Much the same happened to both Americans and Japanese in late 1941. They

3. American Institute of Public Opinion press release, April 30, 1968.

saw their nations as distressingly bound, by a combination of previous acts and factors beyond their control, to a short and not very varied menu. But a much earlier recognition of the constraints on choice and on the prospects for success might have prevented them from becoming boxed in.

I stressed earlier the basic similarity in structure (largely ignoring the labels on the participants) of global politics as it emerged from World War II and what was most likely to have emerged had the United States not fought. The failure of men in high places, now as well as then, to weigh such a view is in large part a failure of political theory and research. Conventional thinking on international politics has, I contend, too much neglected the environment of politics. That is, we have often failed to study the role of social, economic, and technological factors in providing the menu for political choice. Relatively speaking, too much effort has gone into examining the ways in which choices are made, the political process itself, rather than into asking, in a rigorous and systematic way, what possible choices were in fact available and why those possibilities and not some others were available.

I use the term "a macroscopic view," to describe this emphasis on looking at the wider environment within which political decision-makers act. A microscope is of course an instrument for looking in great detail at a tiny portion of tissue or other material, ignoring the whole of a large organism or system for the sake of a painstaking examination of the structure or processes of one element. By contrast, we can use the term macroscope for just the opposite kind of tool, one for examining, in a gross way, the entire system or at least large portions of it. The fine detail available from the microscope is lost, but compensation comes from an image of the interrelationships of the parts. I deliberately use the word macroscope in place of telescope as the opposite for microscope. A telescope is used for making distant objects appear close, for bringing out the detail of distant objects that one cannot approach physically. In this sense its function is not so different from that of the microscope. Like the latter it implies a relatively narrow view; one chooses to focus upon a particular star rather than on the entire galaxy that is visible to the naked eye in the night sky. So what I refer to is more nearly analogous to a wide-angle lens for a camera than to a telephoto lens.

A self-consciously social-scientific study of international politics is crucial to the rigorous use of the macroscopic view, in contrast to the requirements of the earlier emphasis on microscopic analysis of particular events and personalities. The analyst needs to make use of a wide variety of data on the components of international systems, both present and historical systems. Scientific analysis by itself imposes no restrictions on where, that is, at what level of analysis, to develop powerful hypotheses, but it seems especially appropriate for macroscopic analyses. For example, we are just now beginning to see important systematic studies of the patterns of interactions among nations. One scholar is compiling a complete mapping of governments' verbal and physical acts toward other governments in the current international system, and has begun to publish some very important analyses of recent patterns that show unsuspected ways in which the sequence of events in crises is different from that in "normal" times.[4] Other analyses have been concerned with comparative foreign policies, in the sense of how differences in national characteristics affect national policies. These may be relatively small differences, such as between parliamentary and presidential systems, or changes in the structure of particular countries over time, or they may investigate what difference being economically developed, or democratic, or European makes for behavior. Finally, at this same level of aggregation are the patterns of linkages among nations. In-

4. Charles McClelland, "Access to Berlin: The Quantity and Variety of Events, 1948–63," in J. David Singer (ed.) *Quantitative International Politics: Insights and Evidence* (New York: Free Press, 1968) is a preliminary study of these data. See also McClelland and Gary A. Hogard, "Conflict Patterns in the Interactions Among Nations," in James N. Rosenau ed., *International Politics and Foreign Policy* (New York: Free Press, 1969), 2nd ed.

cluded here are studies of trade ties, bonds of communication, and membership in international organizations. Such
studies lead on to comparisons of international systems, de-
fined by a combination of the pattern of linkages plus certain
characteristics of the states being linked. Thus a comparison
of bipolar with multipolar systems depends on measures of
the relative size of the major nations making up the systems,
and the linkages among states that signify the bonds of
alliance.

The power of macroscopic prediction

The aggregate, macroscopic view can be shown to have a
good deal of predictive power. This is so because perceptions,
policy, and capabilities all are quite stable for most nations,
as I will now try to demonstrate. On capabilities, for example,
most nations have changed remarkably little in their *relative*
levels of economic development over the past 60 years. The
rank-order of major countries has varied but slightly since before World War I. Japan has moved up a bit and France down
a couple of notches, but on the whole the rankings of income
levels are about the same as they were, with the United States
at the top followed, in approximately the same order as before, by Sweden, Switzerland, and Canada.[5] In the modern industrial world it is extraordinarily difficult for a nation to
maintain, over a long period of time, a rate of growth that
will enable it to surpass many of its rivals. And it seems almost as hard for a nation to mess up its economy so badly as
to fall very far behind.

On matters of perception and policy the necessary research
did not exist for policy-makers in 1941, and even now the
prewar period is not covered adequately. Nevertheless we can

5. Theodore Caplow, "Are the Poor Countries Getting Poorer?" *Foreign Policy,* 1 no. 3 (Summer 1971): 90–107.

obtain some important information from studies of the post-war world. My initial example will be from work on voting behavior in the United Nations.[6] First, it was found that a very wide variety of particular issues and roll-calls—about the Congo, Korea, Chinese representation, disarmament, South Africa, West New Guinea, and many others—are in fact usually concerned with one of the major broad issues of contemporary world politics. Three great cleavages or "super-issues"—the cold war, colonialism, and the role of the United Nations organization itself—account for about 60 percent of the variation in roll-call voting. This in itself was a surprising regularity. Although United Nations voting is not intrinsically of great importance, governments' behavior there does provide major evidence on their positions in world politics more generally. And most observers would agree that the above are truly the issues around which the entire globe (as contrasted with more parochial regional disputes) currently does divide.

From there it was easy and appropriate to try to predict the voting behavior of particular nations on these superissues. On cold war issues it was possible to predict 75 percent of the variation in voting position by knowing only a few basic facts. Simply categorizing the various states according to regional or caucusing groups would do that well, as would knowing a few facts about the military and economic bonds among nations (their alliance commitments and their receipt of trade and aid from the United States and the Soviet Union.) This too is surprising in view of many predictions that nothing resembling this level of regularity would emerge; that delegates' voting decisions depended too heavily on the vagaries

6. Hayward R. Alker, "Dimensions of Conflict in the General Assembly." *American Political Science Review* 58, no. 3 (September 1964): 642–57; Alker and Bruce M. Russett, *World Politics in the General Assembly* (New Haven, Conn.: Yale University Press, 1965); and Russett, *International Regions and the International System* (Chicago: Rand McNally, 1967), Chapters 4 and 5. See also R. J. Rummel "Some Empirical Findings on Nations and Their Behavior," *World Politics* 21, no. 2 (1969): 226–41.

of instructions from home, or upon volatile interests of the delegations, or interdelegation bargaining, or upon what nation's representative happened to be sitting next to a delegate on a particular day. Furthermore, over 80 percent of the variation in states' voting can be predicted by knowing their *past* voting behavior. Even positions taken ten years previously provide that kind of predictive power.

Votes on smaller, more parochial, and more transient issues are of course more difficult to predict. But on these three continuing and salient cleavages one can do very well at the aggregate, macroscopic level without knowing anything about changing conditions or decision-processes within individual governments. Changes of personnel in the delegations; changes in the leadership of the home governments; alternation of parties; all had little effect. Even changes of regime or governmental structure, as caused by coups or palace revolutions, make little difference to the leaders' perceptions of choice in the United Nations, or at least to their actual choices of behavior. In all but a literal handful of cases it took a virtual social revolution, with an impact on the level of that occurring in Iran with the overthrow of the Mossadegh regime or Guatemala and Arbenz in the 1950s, to produce a very marked shift.

Furthermore, we can specify what we mean by a marked shift. Cuba's change of polarity from Batista to Castro was by far the greatest national flip-flop over the past decade and a half. On a scale of cold war issues, Guatemala and Iran shifted their UN voting by an amount that is roughly one-third of Cuba's change, and there are but six other states that moved by even a fifth as much as Cuba did (not necessarily in the same direction).[7] In most instances one could "map" the political differences and concurrences of nations in a very stable way.

Whatever the *domestic* consequences, even such important revolutions as those in Iraq in 1958 (when the king was overthrown and killed) and Argentina in 1955 (the political end

7. Russett, *International Regions,* pp. 90–91.

of Peron) did not have great impact on their nations' *international* alignments. Iraq withdrew from the Baghdad Pact and bought arms from the Soviet Union, but did not otherwise alter its policies so very greatly. Even the most publicized change of regime in recent years, the rise of Gaullism and of Republic number five, did not affect France's international alignment more than marginally. Seen through the microscopic eye of contemporary American reporting, France's new independent policy seemed to make a great difference in Western Europe and French relations with the Communist states. But on the basic alignments that have characterized international behavior over the past two decades Paris did not deviate significantly. It remained as it had been: anti-Communist on most of the critical cold war issues, sympathetic with its fellow colonial and excolonial powers, and resistant to efforts to strengthen the United Nations' feeble powers to coerce its members.

Similarly, recent work on regional groupings found that knowing international organization memberships ten years previously, or trading patterns ten years previously, allowed one to predict between 85 and 95 percent of the variation in the later period. In the case of trade, one could predict more than three-quarters of the 1963 variation from the 1938 pattern, despite World War II, the Cold War, and decolonization.[8] These influences, and we include here the very important regional and other bonds of community among nations, change at a glacial pace in this international system. The stabilities of our world are, on examination, very impressive.

Moreover, even the few major shifts turn out to be of less moment than they seemed at the time. The big one, Cuba, stimulated the greatest foreign policy fiasco of the Kennedy administration: the Bay of Pigs invasion. The invasion failed and Cuba remained under Castro, and under a Castro newly-

8. Ibid., Chapters 6–11. Also Russett, "Regional Trading Patterns, 1938–1963," *International Studies Quarterly* 12, no. 4 (December 1968): 360–79.

reinforced in his hostility to the United States. Yet from the perspective of a decade it is hard to contend that the results have been very dire for the United States, despite Cuba's proximity and former economic importance to this country. Few countries, even if they made a sharp switch in the alignments, would greatly alter the global balance of power. Only four countries in the non-Communist world (Japan, West Germany, Britain, and France—none of them undeveloped) have a GNP as large as 10 percent of America's.

Finding these continuities contrasts sharply with the task of day-to-day journalism and impressionism. The journalist's job is to tell us how today is different from yesterday, and to do so in a sufficiently vivid manner to attract and hold our attention. When writing about Anglo-American relations, for instance, a good journalist like Drew Middleton changes his evaluation frequently. He looks at political events, personalities, and personal changes in decision-making positions. Anglo-American relations may improve following a meeting of chiefs-of-state, and deteriorate as a consequence of a new disagreement. However valuable this participant's eye-view can be, one must also try to back up and gain perspective both on how the relations between two states fit into the global pattern of relationships and how they perform over a much longer time-span. A day-to-day journalistic view risks confusing the business cycle with the long-term secular trend in the economy. And at that it is not likely to be analogous to a concentration on the depression and inflation ends of the business cycle, but only on the numerous rather mild fluctuations in between.

There is of course a critical limit to the kind of knowledge we can derive from inductive analyses of stability, and it concerns the difference between prediction and explanation. Inductively-derived patterns can be used for substantial periods of time to predict political behavior. If we know empirically that A is associated with B, we may derive important policy benefits from predicting stability in B as a result of stability in A, without knowing why. But however exciting and important the discovery of high aggregate correlations may be, prediction without "understanding" is vulnerable; when we do not understand why two factors are related our predictions will fail if the relationship shifts. The high degree of association between environmental factors and political ones could be deceptive in future international politics. Only new theory could tell us which regularities would hold and which would be shattered.

In this respect our present understanding of international politics is perhaps comparable to the understanding of American voting behavior achieved by early public opinion analysts. They established that certain demographic characteristics, such as religion, income, and occupation, were highly correlated with partisan choice.[9] These correlations were fairly stable over time, but enough individuals, typically less than 20 percent, changed their votes and so could reverse the outcome of the preceding election. Knowing the gross correlations was not enough to identify the dynamic elements—who would change, and whether the changes would be enough to make a major shift in the state of the system. Yet the earlier findings have been of great value, and it is hard to imagine these later questions being studied in their absence.

Choice in retrospect and future

A macroscopic perspective on the stabilities of world politics has crucial policy implications. Too often observers and policy-makers take alarm at every foreign coup or change of government. The Chicken Little syndrome is widespread. But if important policy reversals in these countries are rare, ex-

9. Paul Lazarsfeld, Bernard Berelson, and Hazel Gaudet, *The People's Choice* (New York: Columbia University Press, 1944) and Bernard Berelson, Paul Lazarsfeld, and William McPhee, *Voting* (Chicago: University of Chicago Press, 1954).

pensive attempts to affect the composition of the next gov-
erning coalition in Boonistan are at best unnecessary, and
more likely a dangerous waste of resources that will ultimately weaken the United States both abroad and domes-
tically. And these stabilities limit the prospects for success in
intervention just as they limit the risks of avoiding intervention. Even a power so great as the United States cannot
readily produce in a foreign land a government that will be
notably pro-American unless the necessary social and political
substructure is present.

As children of modern psychology we all are well aware of
the limitations on our personal choice as individuals—limitations of genetic endowment, of environment, and of experience. Without accepting a rigidly deterministic model of
human action, we nevertheless comprehend the severe restrictions within which our private choice is able to move.
Yet we perceive less clearly what are the bounds on the
public choice exercised by leaders of nations; we too often
fail to consider their real options, either as might be seen by
an objective observer or as seen by the decision-maker himself.

If it is true that political choice is severely circumscribed,
we must focus attention on a particular kind of choice node,
on those decisions which sharply restrict the menu of future
options. Often choices are not irreversible, and one may at
least approximate, at a later point, an option that was rejected earlier. For this kind of situation the adage about any
decision being better than no decision, or a paralysis of will,
is applicable. But this happens less often than we may like
to think. In too many circumstances as we proceed from one
node to another previous options become irrecoverable.
Japanese leaders in 1941 found that successive choices cost
them so many alternatives that in the end the decision to
fight the United States, in a war they did not really expect
to win, seemed unavoidable. The American decision to develop atomic weapons brought technical knowledge that cannot be unlearned, immensely complicating disarmament

efforts. The Red Army, whose incursion into Central Europe for the defeat of Hitler we applauded, became less welcome in a changed international system. The decision to fight a "limited" war now may be at the expense of later economic growth, with the consequence that a nation's material power base is forever smaller than it might have been had armaments not taken the place of capital investment. The entry of America into World War II was irreversible; a policy better designed to stay out could, I have contended, have been reversed without irrecoverable damage to this country.

This is an especially serious problem in international politics because we know so little about the articulated consequences of our decisions. Neither the best theorist nor the most confident man of action can really know what the ramifications of an act will be. And the danger is compounded by the speed with which decisions often are forced upon leaders before even whatever inadequate analytical tools we have can be brought to bear on the choice. Scientific and technological advances that now bring the entire world within reach of instantaneous communication, or any target on the globe within 30 minutes of destruction, can leave little time for reflection. When population natural increase rates are two percent a year, total population doubles in thirty years. A world whose population has once reached three billion will never again be the natural, uncrowded environment that our ancestors knew. The further environmental consequences of a jump from 3 billion to 6 billion on earth are far different from those of a jump from 3 million to 6 million. There are also unimagined consequences of the level of power available to change our environment. One manifestation is the potential destructiveness of nuclear warfare, but another ostensibly more constructive manifestation is in the changes that modern industrial processes and urban living patterns are inflicting on the environment. We face an "ecological crisis" from pollutants that could quite literally make the globe uninhabitable.

Hence the old virtues of any decision being better than none become transmuted. The avoidance of a decision that would work irreversible changes looks attractive if there is some chance that we can, with time, better evaluate the consequences of decision.

Japan's 1941 policy is a good example of how hard it may be to recognize critical decision nodes when they do appear. America's incremental creep into the Vietnam quagmire is another. Regrettably, there is no automatic warning signal to flash before the decision-maker. For now, perhaps all one can do to identify such nodes before they are passed is always to have someone ask explicitly, "What will it cost if this decision turns out badly? How, if at all, could we turn back?" This scepticism might help prevent seduction by alternatives that seem to carry fairly high probabilities of favorable outcomes, and high benefits if they work, but disastrous costs should they fail. The acquisition of very expensive weapons systems (because their costs will foreclose other military or civilian options) is an especially relevant class, as is the procurement of systems with very greatly enhanced capabilities. So, in this world, is a superpower's decision actually to use military force. And so, perhaps unfortunately, would be a decision to implement a major disarmament measure. In the last case, however, our foreign policy-making system is well supplied with cautionary voices; for the others the devil's advocate has too often been reticent or unwelcome.

Politics, it sometimes seems, has become the arena for avoiding cataclysm. Political gladiators can destroy far more readily than they can create; their task is one of avoiding error. But they are human, and in repeated encounters ultimately they do blunder. It may be more fruitful to ask what shapes the arena than what determines each stroke of their blunt swords.

This point of view also puts into better perspective the questions that have been raised specifically about Franklin Roosevelt's wisdom. Many readers will conclude that ideally perhaps America should have stayed out of the war, but for reasons of domestic politics or limited visionary powers the option really was not available. That, however, does *not* excuse us from raising the question. As it happens, it is likely that most other men who might have occupied his position would have behaved similarly. Certainly had Wendell Willkie won the presidential election of 1940 it is hard to imagine the ultimate outcome being very different. The anti-interventionists of the time had another vision of America's interests and dangers, but they failed, especially as the wars in China and Europe dragged on, to sustain their case. They too generally lacked both well-developed theory and empirical evidence on which to build their case that the global environment was not as threatening to America as the interventionists believed. Thus the political basis for a delicate policy of all-out aid short of all-out war, if it had ever existed, had eroded by late 1941. The lack of an adequate intellectual basis played no small part in the failure to develop a viable political course.

Now Americans are again, in large numbers, questioning the moral and intellectual basis of interventionist policies pursued by the American government over the past quarter of a century. Others fear that the emotional reaction against those policies will be so strong as to lead to a new isolationism. To such people it may seem virtual treason to risk assisting that reaction by questioning American participation in World War II—a matter on which, as I granted at the outset of this book, the approving case is appreciably stronger than it is for many more recent American interventions. But a reasoned questioning, leading all of us to rethink our premises and search out new evidence, is required if we are to make wise political choices in a new era.

As Robert Penn Warren once put it, "Man is conceived in sin and born in corruption." Less theologically, injustice will always remain in the world. Americans can, by judicious use of their abilities, somewhat diminish the amount of that injustice. But attempts to oppose injustice everywhere by military means will simply destroy our own polity, economy, and society, bringing greater injustice nearer at hand. Americans are neither omnipotent nor omniscient. As I have said earlier,

> Military force becomes Tolkien's One Ring of Power. On occasion we must wield that power to defend ourselves and our friends and to keep the Ring from passing to our enemies. . . . Yet employment of the Ring must be rare and restricted to cases of great necessity. Used rashly, unworthily, or even often, it will corrupt its bearer. Perhaps the United States, by its history and its ideals, carries some limited degree of immunity to the Ring's curse. But excessive reliance on force will quickly weaken, not strengthen us, and ultimately we will be no better than those we oppose.[10]

When contemplating intervention in another land or distant war the following questions should first be answered as precisely as possible:

1. How bad an outcome, by whatever criteria, really is likely if American intervention does not occur?

2. How likely—highly probable or only a long-shot—is it that such a bad outcome will in fact happen?

3. What favorable outcome really is likely as a result of the contemplated intervention?

4. How likely is it that such a good outcome will in fact be produced?

5. At what cost—political, material, and moral—would the outcome probably be achieved? Would success be worth the price?

---

10. Russett, *What Price Vigilance?*, pp. 183–84.

Index